MW01492573

Taking An ASE Certification Test

This study guide will help prepare you to take and pass the ASE test. It contains descriptions of the types of questions used on the test, the task list from which the test questions are derived, a review of the task list subject information, and a practice test containing ASE style questions.

ABOUT ASE

The National Institute for Automotive Service Excellence (ASE) is a non-profit organization founded in 1972 for the purpose of improving the quality of automotive service and repair through the voluntary testing and certification of automotive technicians. Currently, there are over 400,000 professional technicians certified by ASE in over 40 different specialist areas.

ASE certification recognizes your knowledge and experience, and since it is voluntary, taking and passing an ASE certification test also demonstrates to employers and customers your commitment to your profession. It can mean better compensation and increased employment opportunities as well.

ASE not only certifies technician competency, it also promotes the benefits of technician certification to the motoring public. Repair shops that employ at least one ASE technician can display the ASE sign. Establishments where 75 percent of technicians are certified, with at least one technician certified in each area of service offered by the business, are eligible for the ASE Blue Seal of Excellence program. ASE encourages consumers to patronize these shops through media campaigns and car care clinics.

To become ASE certified, you must pass at least one ASE exam and have at least two years of related work experience. Technicians that pass specified tests in a series earn Master Technician status. Your cer-

tification is valid for five years, after which time you must retest to retain certification, demonstrating that you have kept up with the changing technology in the field.

THE ASE TEST

An ASE test consists of forty to eighty multiple-choice questions. Test questions are written by a panel of technical experts from vehicle, parts and equipment manufacturers, as well as working technicians and technical education instructors. All questions have been pre-tested and quality checked on a national sample of technicians. The questions are derived from information presented in the task list, which details the knowledge that a technician must have to pass an ASE test and be recognized as competent in that category. The task list is periodically updated by ASE in response to changes in vehicle technology and repair techniques.

Customer Service 1-800-497-0037
e-mail: PassTheASE@endeavorb2b.com
URL: www.PassTheASE.com
T4 - MEDIUM/HEAVY-DUTY BRAKES

There are five types of questions on an ASE test:
- Direct, or Completion
- MOST likely
- Technician A and Technician B
- EXCEPT
- LEAST likely

Direct, or Completion

This type of question is the kind that is most familiar to anyone who has taken a multiple-choice test: you must answer a direct question or complete a statement with the correct answer. There are four choices given as potential answers, but only one is correct. Sometimes the correct answer to one of these questions is clear, however in other cases more than one answer may seem to be correct. In that case, read the question carefully and choose the answer that is most correct. Here is an example of this type of test question:

A compression test shows that one cylinder is too low. A leakage test on that cylinder shows that there is excessive leakage. During the test, air could be heard coming from the tailpipe. Which of the following could be the cause?
A. broken piston rings
B. bad head gasket
C. bad exhaust gasket
D. an exhaust valve not seating

There is only one correct answer to this question, answer D. If an exhaust valve is not seated, air will leak from the combustion chamber by way of the valve out to the tailpipe and make an audible sound. Answer C is wrong because an exhaust gasket has nothing to do with combustion chamber sealing. Answers A and B are wrong because broken rings or a bad head gasket would have air leaking through the oil filler or coolant system.

MOST Likely

This type of question is similar to a direct question but it can be more challenging because all or some of the answers may be nearly correct. However, only one answer is the most correct. For example:

When a cylinder head with an overhead camshaft is discovered to be warped, which of the following is the most correct repair option?
A. replace the head
B. check for cracks, straighten the head, surface the head
C. surface the head, then straighten it
D. straighten the head, surface the head, check for cracks

The most correct answer is B. It makes no sense to perform repairs on a cylinder head that might not be usable. The head should first be checked for warpage and cracks. Therefore, answer B is more correct than answer D. The head could certainly be replaced, but the cost factor may be prohibitive and availability may be limited, so answer B is more correct than answer A. If the top of the head is warped enough to interfere with cam bore alignment and/or restrict free movement of the camshaft, the head must be straightened before it is resurfaced, so answer C is wrong.

Technician A and Technician B

These questions are the kind most commonly associated with the ASE test. With these questions you are asked to choose which technician statement is correct, or whether they both are correct or incorrect. This type of question can be difficult because very often you may find one technician's statement to be clearly correct or incorrect while the other may not be so obvious. Do you choose one technician or both? The key to answering these questions is to carefully examine each technician's statement independently and judge it on its own merit. Here is an example of this type of question:

A vehicle equipped with rack-and-pinion steering is having the front end inspected. Technician A says that the inner tie rod ends should be inspected while in their normal running position. Technician B says that if movement is felt between the tie rod stud and the socket while the tire is moved in and out, the inner tie rod should be replaced. Who is correct?
A. Technician A
B. Technician B
C. Both A and B
D. Neither A or B

The correct answer is C; both technicians' statements are correct. Technician B is clearly correct because any play felt between the tie-rod stud and the socket while the tire is moved in and out indicates that the assembly is worn and requires replacement. However, Technician A is also correct because inner tie- rods should be inspected while in their normal running position, to prevent binding that may occur when the suspension is allowed to hang free.

EXCEPT

This kind of question is sometimes called a negative question because you are asked to give the incorrect answer. All of the possible answers given are correct EXCEPT one. In effect, the correct answer to the question is the one that is wrong. The word EXCEPT is always capitalized in these questions. For example:
All of the following are true of torsion bars **EXCEPT**:
A. They can be mounted longitudinally or transversely.

B. They serve the same function as coil springs.

C. They are interchangeable from side-to-side

D. They can be used to adjust vehicle ride height.

The correct answer is C. Torsion bars are not normally interchangeable from side-to-side. This is because the direction of the twisting or torsion is not the same on the left and right sides. All of the other answers contain true statements regarding torsion bars.

LEAST Likely

This type of question is similar to EXCEPT in that once again you are asked to give the answer that is wrong. For example:

Blue-gray smoke comes from the exhaust of a vehicle during deceleration. Of the following, which cause is **LEAST** likely?

A. worn valve guides

B. broken valve seals

C. worn piston rings

D. clogged oil return passages

The correct answer is C. Worn piston rings will usually make an engine smoke worse under acceleration. All of the other causes can allow oil to be drawn through the valve guides under the high intake vacuum that occurs during deceleration.

PREPARING FOR THE ASE TEST

Begin preparing for the test by reading the task list. The task list describes the actual work performed by a technician in a particular specialty area. Each question on an ASE test is derived from a task or set of tasks in the list. Familiarizing yourself with the task list will help you to concentrate on the areas where you need to study.

The text section of this study guide contains information pertaining to each of the tasks in the task list. Reviewing this information will prepare you to take the practice test.

Take the practice test and compare your answers with the correct answer explanations. If you get an answer wrong and don't understand why, go back and read the information pertaining to that question in the text.

After reviewing the tasks and the subject information and taking the practice test, you should be prepared to take the ASE test or be aware of areas where further study is needed. When studying with this study guide or any other source of information, use the following guidelines to make sure the time spent is as productive as possible:

- Concentrate on the subject areas where you are weakest.
- Arrange your schedule to allow specific times for studying.
- Study in an area where you will not be distracted.
- Don't try to study after a full meal or when you are tired.
- Don't wait until the last minute and try to 'cram' for the test.

REGISTERING FOR ASE COMPUTER-BASED TESTING

Registration for the ASE CBT tests can be done online in myASE or over the phone. While not mandatory, it is recommended that you establish a myASE account on the ASE website (www.ase.com). This can be a big help in managing the ASE certification process, as your test scores and certification expiry dates are all listed there.

Test times are available during two-month windows with a one-month break in between. This means that there is a total of eight months over the period of the calendar year that ASE testing is available.

Testing can be scheduled during the daytime, night, and weekends for maximum flexibility. Also, results are available immediately after test completion. Printed certificates are mailed at the end of the two-month test window. If you fail a test, you will not be allowed to register for the same test until the next two-month test window.

TAKING THE ASE TEST – COMPUTER-BASED TESTING (CBT)

On test day, bring some form of photo identification with you and be sure to arrive at the test center 30 minutes early to give sufficient time to check in. Once you have checked in, the test supervisor will issue you some scratch paper and pencils, as well as a composite vehicle test booklet if you are taking advanced tests. You will then be seated at a computer station and given a short online tutorial on how to complete the ASE CBT tests. You may skip the tutorial if you are already familiar with the CBT process.

The test question format is similar to those found in written ASE tests. Regular certification tests have a time limit of 1 to 2 hours, depending on the test. Recertification tests are 30 to 45 minutes, and the L1 and L2 advanced level tests are capped at 2 hours. The time remaining for your test is displayed on the top left of the test window. You are given a warning when you have 5 minutes left to complete the test.

Read through each question carefully. If you don't know the answer to a question and need to think about it, click on the "Flag" button and move on to the next question. You may also go back to previous questions by pressing the "Previous Question" button. Don't sspend too much time on any one question. After you have worked through to the end of the test, check your remaining time and go back and answer the questions you flagged. Very often, information found in questions later in the test can help answer some of the ones with which you had difficulty.

Some questions may have more content than what can fit on one screen. If this is the case, there will be a "More" button displayed where the "Next Question" button would ordinarily appear. A scrolling bar will also appear, showing what part of the question you are currently viewing. Once you have viewed all of the related content for the question, the "Next Question" button will reappear.

You can change answers on any of the questions before submitting the test for scoring. At the end of the examination, you will be shown a table with all of the question numbers. This table will show which questions are answered, which are unanswered, and which have been flagged for review. You will be given the option to review all the questions, review the flagged questions, or review the unanswered questions from this page. This table can be reviewed at any time during the exam by clicking the "Review" button.

If you are running out of time and still have unanswered test questions, guess the answers if necessary to make sure every question is answered. Do not leave any answers blank. It is to your advantage to answer every question, because your test score is based on the number of correct answers. A guessed answer could be correct, but a blank answer can never be.

Once you are satisfied that all of the questions are complete and ready for scoring, click the "Submit for Scoring" button. If you are scheduled for more than one test, the next test will begin immediately. If you are done with testing, you will be asked to complete a short survey regarding the CBT test experience. As you are leaving the test center, your supervisor will give you a copy of your test results. Your scores will also be available on myASE within two business days.

To learn exactly where and when the ASE Certification Tests are available in your area, as well as the costs involved in becoming ASE certified, please contact ASE directly for registration information.

The National Institute for Automotive Service Excellence
101 Blue Seal Drive, S.E. Suite 101
Leesburg, VA 20175
1-800-390-6789
http://www.ase.com

Table of Contents
T4 - Medium/Heavy-Duty Brakes

Test Specifications And Task List 6

Air Brakes Diagnosis And Repair 9

Hydraulic Brakes Diagnosis And Repair 37

**Air And Hydraulic Antilock Brake Systems (ABS) And Automatic
Traction Control (ATC), Electronic Stability Control Systems** 51

Sample Test Questions 58

Answers To Sample Test Questions 66

Glossary 75

Medium/Heavy-Duty Brakes
TEST SPECIFICATIONS
FOR MEDIUM/HEAVY-DUTY BRAKES
(TEST T4)

CONTENT AREA		NUMBER OF QUESTIONS IN ASE TEST	PERCENTAGE OF COVERAGE IN ASE TEST
A. Air Brakes Diagnosis And Repair		33	66%
1. Air Supply And Service Systems	(16)		
2. Mechanical/Foundation	(13)		
3. Parking Brakes	(4)		
B. Hydraulic Brakes Diagnosis And Repair		12	24%
C. Air and Hydraulic Antilock Brake System (ABS) And Automatic Traction Control (ATC), Electronic Stability Control Systems		5	10%
Total		**50**	**100%**

There could be up to ten additional questions that are included for statistical research purposes only. Your answers to these questions will not affect your test score, but since you do not know which ones they are, you should answer all questions in the test.

The 5-year Recertification Test will cover the same content areas as those listed above. However, the number of questions in each content area of the Recertification Test will be reduced by about one-half.

The following pages list the tasks covered in each content area. These task descriptions offer detailed information to technicians preparing for the test and persons who may be instructing Medium/Heavy-Duty Brakes technicians. This task list may also serve as a guideline for question writers, reviewers and test assemblers.

It should be noted that the number of questions in each content area might not equal the number of tasks listed. Some of the tasks are complex and broad in scope, and may be covered by several questions. Other tasks are simple and narrow in scope; one question may cover several tasks. The main purpose for listing the tasks is to describe accurately what is done on the job, not to make each task correspond to a particular test question.

MEDIUM/HEAVY-DUTY BRAKES TEST TASK LIST

A. AIR BRAKES DIAGNOSIS AND REPAIR
(33 QUESTIONS)

1. AIR SUPPLY AND SERVICE SYSTEMS
(16 QUESTIONS)

Task 1 – Review driver/vehicle inspection report (DVIR); verify the complaint and road test vehicle; review driver/customer interview and past maintenance documents (if available); determine further diagnosis.

Task 2 - Check air system build-up time; check air system air loss rate (leakage); determine needed repairs.

Task 3 – Inspect, test, repair or replace air pressure gauges, in-cab lines, hoses, fittings, and pressure sensors (transducers).

Task 4 – Inspect, test, and replace low pressure warning devices.

Task 5 – Drain air reservoir tanks; check for oil, water, and foreign material; determine needed repairs.

Task 6 – Inspect, adjust, align, and replace compressor drive belts and pulleys.

Task 7 – Inspect and replace compressor drive gear and coupling.

Task 8 – Inspect, repair, or replace air compressor, air inlet supply, oil supply, water lines, hoses, fittings and mounting brackets.

Task 9 – Inspect, test, adjust, and replace system pressure controls (governor/relief valve), unloader assembly, lines, hoses, and fittings.

Task 10 - Inspect, repair, or replace air system lines, hoses, fittings, and couplings; check for proper routing and mounting.

Task 11 - Inspect, test, clean,

and replace air tank relief (pop off) valves, one-way (single) check valves, drain valves, automatic drain (spitter) valves, heaters, wiring, and connectors.

Task 12 - Inspect, test, clean, repair, or replace air dryer systems, filters, valves, heaters, wiring, and connectors.

Task 13 - Inspect, test, and replace brake application (foot) valve, fittings, and mounts; check pedal operation.

Task 14 - Inspect, test, repair, or replace stop and parking brake light circuit switches, wiring, and connectors.

Task 15 - Inspect, test, repair, or replace hand brake (trailer) control valve, lines, hoses, fittings, and mountings.

Task 16 - Inspect, test, and replace brake relay valves, quick relay valves, and anti-compounding circuits.

Task 17 - Inspect, test, and replace tractor protection valve.

Task 18 - Inspect, test, and replace inversion/emergency (spring) brake control valve(s).

Task 19 - Determine if air brake system problem is caused by tractor or trailer supply or service system components.

2. MECHANICAL/FOUNDATION AND WHEEL HUB
(13 QUESTIONS)

Task 1 - Diagnose poor stopping, premature wear, brake noise, pulling, grabbing, or dragging problems caused by foundation brake components; determine needed repairs.

Task 2 - Inspect, test, and replace service brake chambers, diaphragms, clamps, return springs, pushrods, clevises, and mounting brackets.

Task 3 - Inspect, service, and replace automatic slack adjusters.

Task 4 - Inspect and replace S-cam brake rollers, bushings, camshafts, seals, spacers, retainers, brake spiders, shields, anchor pins, and springs.

Task 5 - Inspect, clean, adjust, and replace air disc brake caliper

assemblies.

Task 6 - Inspect brake shoes or pads; determine needed repairs.

Task 7 - Replace brake shoes or pads; determine correct replacement lining/pad coefficient of friction rating for application.

Task 8 - Inspect and replace brake drums or rotors as needed.

Task 9 - Clean, inspect, lubricate, and replace wheel hubs, wheel bearings and races/cups; replace seals and wear rings; adjust wheel bearings (including one and two nut types) to manufacturers' specifications.

Task 10 - Inspect and replace unitized hub bearing assemblies; perform initial installation and maintenance procedures to manufacturers' specifications.

3. PARKING BRAKES
(4 QUESTIONS)

Task 1 - Inspect and test parking (spring) brake chambers operation to include spring condition, leakage, and installation/mounting.

Task 2 - Replace parking (spring) brake chambers; dispose of chambers in accordance with local regulations.

Task 3 - Inspect, test, and replace parking (spring) brake valves, lines, hoses, and fittings.

Task 4 - Inspect, test, and replace parking (spring) brake dash control valve.

Task 5 - Manually release (cage) and set (uncage) parking (spring) brakes.

B. HYDRAULIC BRAKES DIAGNOSIS AND REPAIR
(12 QUESTIONS)

Task 1 - Diagnose poor stopping, brake noise, premature wear, pulling, grabbing, dragging, or pedal feel problems caused by hydraulic system components; determine needed repairs.

Task 2 - Pressure test hydraulic system and inspect for fluid leaks; check system pressure actuator operation, and diagnose fault codes using a PC computer if applicable.

Task 3 - Check brake pedal operation and adjust free play.

Task 4 - Inspect, test, and replace master cylinder; check pushrod length.

Task 5 - Inspect and replace brake lines, flexible hoses, and fittings; check for proper routing and mounting.

Task 6 - Inspect, test, and replace metering (hold off), load sensing/proportioning, proportioning, and combination valves.

Task 7 - Inspect, test, repair, or replace brake pressure differential valve and warning light circuits, switches, bulbs, wiring, and connectors.

Task 8 - Inspect and replace wheel cylinders.

Task 9 - Inspect, service, and replace disc brake caliper assemblies.

Task 10 - Inspect/test brake fluid; bleed and/or flush system; determine proper fluid type for application.

Task 11 - Diagnose poor stopping, brake noise, premature wear, pulling, grabbing, dragging, or pedal feel problems caused by disc and drum brake mechanical components; determine needed repairs.

Task 12 - Inspect and replace brake drums or rotors; resurface rotors if applicable.

Task 13 - Inspect, adjust, and replace brake shoes, mounting hardware, adjuster mechanisms, and backing plates.

Task 14 - Inspect, service, and replace brake pads, hardware, and mounts.

Task 15 - Inspect, adjust, and replace drive line parking brake system components.Task 2 - Inspect, resurface or replace brake drums or rotors.

Task 16 - Diagnose poor stopping complaints caused by brake assist (booster) system problems; determine needed repairs; (includes hydraulic and hydraulic/electric assist systems).

Task 17 - Inspect, test, repair, or replace power brake assist (booster), hoses, control valves and filters; determine proper fluid type for application.

Task 18 - Test, adjust, repair or replace brake stop light switch, bulbs, wiring, and connectors.

C. AIR AND HYDRAULIC ANTILOCK BRAKE SYSTEMS (ABS) AND AUTOMATIC TRACTION CONTROL (ATC), ELECTRONIC STABILITY CONTROL SYSTEMS
(5 QUESTIONS)

Task 1 - Observe antilock brake system (ABS) operation, self test operation and warning light operation; determine if further diagnosis is needed; (includes dash mounted trailer ABS warning light).

Task 2 - Diagnose antilock brake system (ABS) electronic controls and components using self-diagnosis (blink codes) and/or specified test equipment (scan tool, PC based software); determine needed repairs.

Task 3 - Diagnose poor stopping and wheel lock-up caused by failure of the antilock brake system (ABS); determine needed repairs.

Task 4 - Inspect, test, and replace antilock brake system (ABS) air, hydraulic, electrical, and mechanical components.

Task 5 - Diagnose automatic traction control (ATC) electronic control(s) and components using self-diagnosis (blink codes) and/or specified test equipment (scan tool, PC based software); determine needed repairs.

Task 6 - Diagnose electronic stability control systems and components

We employ technicians certified by the
National Institute for
AUTOMOTIVE
SERVICE
EXCELLENCE
Let us show you their credentials

using self-diagnosis (blink codes) and/or specified test equipment (scan tool, PC based software); determine needed repairs.

The preceding Task List details all of the related informational subject matter you are expect to know in order to sit for this ASE Certification Test. Your own years of experience as a technician in the professional automotive service repair trade also should provide you with added background.

Finally, a conscientious review of the self-study material provided in this Training for ASE Certification unit also should help you to be adequately prepared to take this test.

NOTE: The procedures contained in this book are intended to give you an overview of typical air and hydraulic brake inspection, service and repair. Model-specific overhaul procedures, specifications and tolerances may vary depending on the particular component manufacturer.

Air Brakes Diagnosis and Repair

SAFETY

Always use extreme caution when working on air brake systems:

- Always make sure the truck is parked on a level surface and make sure the wheels are blocked
- Make sure the engine and/or air compressor is disabled
- Make sure all air is completely drained from the system before servicing
- If necessary, disconnect the electrical system
- Never disconnect/reconnect a hose or line with air pressure in the system
- Use replacement parts that are authorized by the Original Equipment Manufacturer (OEM)
- Always replace damaged components.

DRIVER VEHICLE INSPECTION REPORT (DVIR)

According to Federal Motor Vehicle Safety Standards (FMVSS), truck drivers are required to prepare and submit a DVIR to their motor carrier or owner at the end of each day. The DVIR is to be retained by the owner of the vehicle, and is used to identify defects or deficiencies that would result in a mechanical breakdown or effect the safe operation of a vehicle. Once a driver submits the DVIR, a motor carrier or its agent must investigate and repair the defect or deficiency.

Inspect the DVIR, paying particular attention to any noted mechanical concerns. Keep in mind that a failure that may seem like it's in the brake system could actually be in the steering or suspension system.

Reaffirm the complaint by getting as much information as possible from the driver. Remember, the driver is sometimes the best link in the diagnostic chain. Carefully question the driver about the symptoms, when they occur, and how long they have been occurring. What is the driver doing when he or she experiences the problem? Is there a temperature, running time, time spent without running, particular speed, or road condition prerequisite?

If possible, check the vehicle service history. Look for similar complaints in the past, and look up any known Technical Service Bulletins (TSB) that would reveal factory recalls, service campaigns, or updated repair information regarding the symptom(s) in question. Thorough research at this point could save valuable time that can be used to expedite the repair process.

AIR SUPPLY AND SERVICE SYSTEMS

Supply system

Supply system component malfunctions can be the cause of many brake performance problems.

The inspection of a truck's brake system may require one or more road tests. Typically, the first time a road test is needed is to verify any unusual characteristics that can be followed up by performing the in-shop inspection. By road testing the vehicle prior to the scheduled inspection, you will have a better chance of identifying potential problems of which the driver may not be aware. As you drive, be sensitive to the way all the controls feel, not just those outlined on the driver's report.

Start the engine and check for proper operation of all the instruments, gauges, and warning lights, paying particular attention to the air pressure gauge(s). This is not only important for braking system inspection, but also ensures that the vehicle is safe to road test. As the engine is running at idle, air pressure should build up according to specification.

Next, give the vehicle a thorough road test. If the vehicle's brakes are not applying and releasing properly, grabbing or dragging, defective supply system components could be the cause. Remember, a 4-psi difference in air delivery between axles is enough to cause instability and premature wear.

When you get back to the shop, check the operation of the parking brake. Also, make sure the parking brake indicator light on the dash comes on.

If all-around braking performance is poor or if the system is not building up enough air pressure, look for signs such as a clogged compressor air filter, slipping belt (if equipped), air leaks, restricted lines, a defective governor, or even a malfunctioning air compressor.

If system pressure is too high, suspect a defective governor or reservoir safety valve. Check the governor's cut-out pressure. It may be too high, causing system over-pressurization. Also, the reservoir safety valve may not be allowing excessive pressure to be purged from the air tanks.

Pressure Drop

Start the engine and allow the air system to build up to its governed specification (usually between 120-130 psi). Next, shut off the engine.

Release the service brakes and time the air pressure drop. The loss rate should be less than 2 psi/minute for straight trucks and less than 3 psi/minute for combination vehicles. Next, apply the service brakes to at least 90 psi and time the pressure drop. (Don't count the initial drop when you hit the pedal). The loss rate should be less than 3 psi/minute for straight trucks and less than 4 psi/minute for combination vehicles.

Air Pressure Gauges

Trucks with air brakes come equipped with pressure gauges mounted on the dash. These gauges will indicate how much air pressure is in the system at any given time. Drivers must train themselves to periodically inspect the gauges for any abnormal pressure readings, and to report those abnormalities to the

technician. When system pressures fall below 60 psi, either a warning light will illuminate, or a buzzer will sound (maybe both).

Gauges are available in either individual or dual-gauge configurations. Note that system pressures fluctuate while the vehicle is being operated. Some systems include a separate application gauge, which can inform the driver of specific pressure when the brakes are applied.

Dash air pressure gauges operate on the principle of changing an air brake pressure signal into an electronic voltage signal. An element inside an air pressure transducer responds to air pressure increase or decrease, and the transducer converts that pressure differentiation into a voltage signal, which is displayed in a proportionate reading

on the dash gauge.

To check the transducer and gauge assembly, make sure the air supply value is within manufacturer's specifications. Next, inspect the transducer output voltage and compare with manufacturer's specifications. If the transducer voltage output is not within normal readings, suspect a defective transducer. If the transducer voltage output is within normal readings, suspect a defective gauge. Always inspect hoses, lines, fittings, and replace as necessary.

Low-Pressure Warning Device

A defective low-pressure warning device will fail to signal the driver of diminished air pressure in the brake system. The low-pressure warning indicator is installed on the primary reservoir,

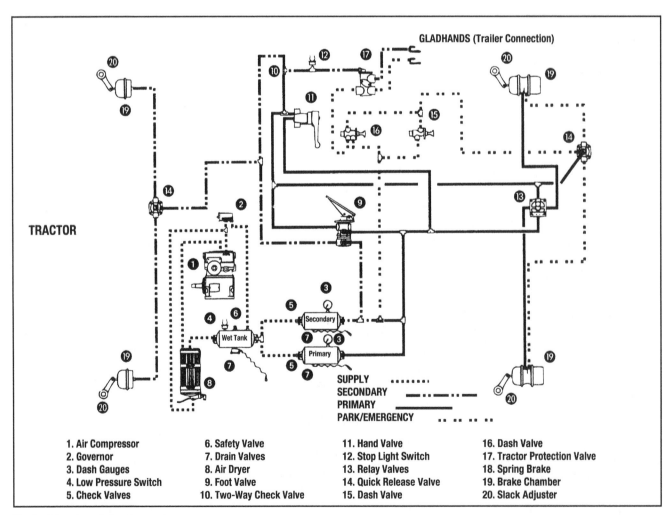

Typical tractor air brake system.

1. Air Compressor
2. Governor
3. Dash Gauges
4. Low Pressure Switch
5. Check Valves
6. Safety Valve
7. Drain Valves
8. Air Dryer
9. Foot Valve
10. Two-Way Check Valve
11. Hand Valve
12. Stop Light Switch
13. Relay Valves
14. Quick Release Valve
15. Dash Valve
16. Dash Valve
17. Tractor Protection Valve
18. Spring Brake
19. Brake Chamber
20. Slack Adjuster

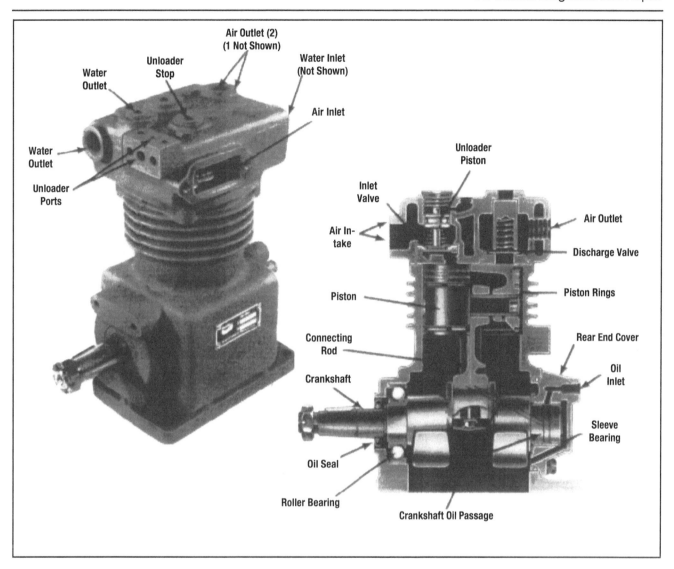

Single-cylinder compressor. *(Courtesy: Bendix Corp.)*

and notifies the operator of system air depletion. Once pressure falls below 60 psi, contacts inside the warning device close, completing the circuit and activating a warning buzzer, instrument panel light, or in some cases both.

To check operation of the indicator, completely depressurize the air brake system (key on engine off) by pumping the brake pedal multiple times. When pressure in the system is depleted to approximately 60 psi, observe that the indicator signals operate. If the indicator signals do not operate, check for voltage at the warning device. If the circuit is open, suspect a defective low-pressure warning device. As with any electronic failure, always inspect all wiring and connections.

To replace the low-pressure warning device, completely depressurize the air brake system, remove the air lines, and unscrew from the primary reservoir.

Air Reservoir Inspection

The supply reservoir or 'wet tank' is the one closest to the compressor. This reservoir feeds air to the primary and secondary reservoirs of the air brake system. When the brake pedal is depressed, air flows from the primary reservoir,

Four-cylinder compressor. *(Courtesy: Bendix Corp.)*

through the primary section of the foot valve, and out to the rear foundation brakes. Meanwhile, at the same time, air flows from the secondary reservoir through the secondary section of the foot valve to actuate the front foundation brakes.

Inspect the air tank reservoirs, noting any damage that may have been caused by road debris. Inspect air reservoir mounting, taking into consideration adequate clearance for other components such as power take off assemblies and brake lines. Check all lines, fittings, and valves for damage and replace as necessary.

Compressor

A malfunctioning air compressor can develop air leaks and pass oil into the brake system, which in turn will cause poor stopping, grabbing or dragging.

Although there are many other components in the air brake system, the one that bears the heaviest burden is the air compressor. When the air enters the compressor cylinder, it is compressed and forced through a discharge valve to the supply reservoir.

A single-cylinder or two-cylinder compressor is used for most truck applications. However, three and four-cylinder air compressors are available for applications where high air volume is in demand, such as on trucks with multiple trailers and air-powered accessories. Compressors can be liquid cooled–utilizing coolant from the engine–air cooled, or both. Most compressors utilize oil from the truck's engine for lubrication.

Some air compressors even have their own oil sumps. If the compressor is self-lubricated, the oil should be checked daily. If oil is pumped in from the engine compartment, the engine oil should be checked in accordance with the engine manufacturer's scheduled maintenance intervals.

Diagnosis

NOTE: Before diagnosing the sys-

tem, shut off the engine and block the wheels to prevent vehicle movement.

Clean excessive dirt, oil and debris from around the compressor. Compressor mounting bolts must be checked for proper torque, and brackets must not be missing or damaged.

Power is transferred to the compressor by either an internal gear or an external belt, most commonly called an accessory drive belt. If the compressor is belt driven, the belt must be inspected and tightened to manufacturer's specifications.

Check the belts following the manufacturer's recommended intervals for evidence of wear such as cracking, fraying, missing sections, oil contamination and incorrect tension. Also, check for hard objects such as small stones or sand that may become imbedded in the bottom of the belt or in the pulley grooves. Determine the belt tension at a point halfway between the pulleys by pressing on the belt with moderate thumb pressure. Check belt deflection and compare with manufacturer's recommendations.

When replacing the compressor belt, inspect the compressor for looseness and improper alignment. Loosen the belt tensioner or accessory drive pivot, and remove the belt. Never pry the belt from its pulley. After the belt is removed, inspect the pulley to determine if it has any imperfections.

Install a new belt by correctly positioning it in its pulley grooves. Using the proper tools, move the accessory to tighten the belt, or in the case of automatically tensioned drives, move the tensioner to a position where the belt can be installed onto the pulleys. Use the proper tension recommendations and installation tools for the particular application.

A properly aligned pulley system reduces both pulley and belt wear, along with excessive vibration. If the belt pulleys are severely misaligned, look for improper positioning of the air compressor, improper fit of the pul-

ley or shaft, or incorrect accessory drive components. Inspect the pulleys for chips, nicks, cracks, tool marks, bent sidewalls, severe corrosion or other damage. Parallel and angular pulley alignment can be checked using a straightedge.

With the engine running at idle, air pressure should build to 85-100 psi within forty-five seconds. If the engine is running at full-governed rpm, air should build up within twenty-five seconds, and the compressor should maintain a constant pressure. If it does not build up in time, the system must be checked for leaks. If no leaks are found, it is possible that a dirty air filter is restricting the compressor intake.

In addition to a slow air compressor build up time, a plugged filter creates a vacuum in the compressor cylinder during the intake stroke. Oil is then sucked past the compressor's piston rings. On the compression stroke, the piston pumps all of the accumulated oil through the discharge line, and right into the air system. Excessive oil in the air system can gum up major components, causing them to fail prematurely.

It's always a good practice to make checking the air compressor filter a part of a standard PM maintenance program. With air pressure applied to the unloader cavity and with the governor cut out, remove the air filter or the air pick-up tube and check for air leaks by squirting oil around the unloader plunger and stem. If there is leakage, replace the unloader mechanism.

Ensure the system is fully discharged of air and disconnect the discharge line from the compressor. If it's sludged to the point where the inside diameter (ID) is substantially reduced, that's a sign that the compressor is passing excessive oil.

Even with a clean air filter, a compressor can pass oil if oil control rings are excessively worn. Failure to change compressor oil or engine oil (if the compressor shares oil with the engine) is the most common cause of prema-

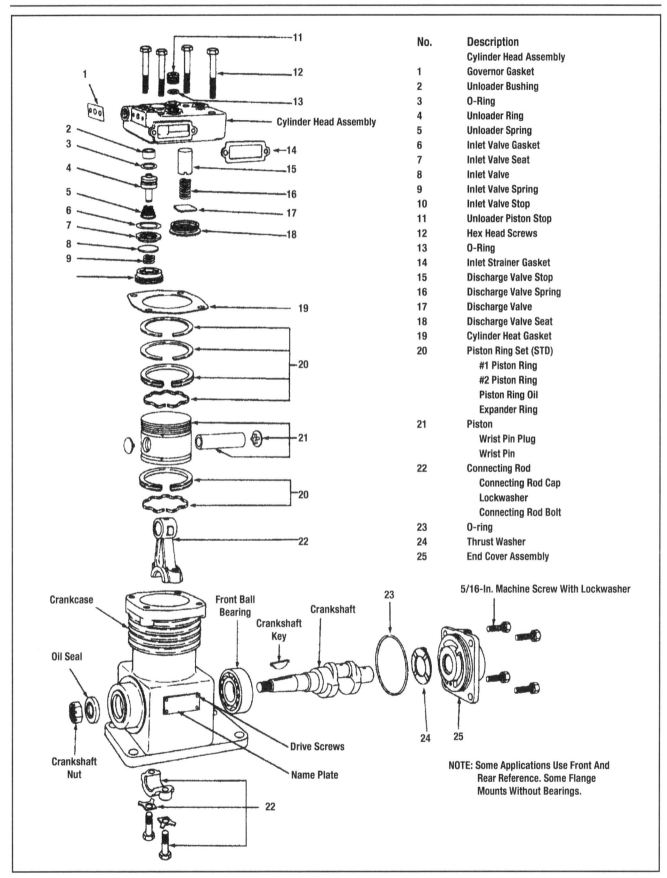

No.	Description
	Cylinder Head Assembly
1	Governor Gasket
2	Unloader Bushing
3	O-Ring
4	Unloader Ring
5	Unloader Spring
6	Inlet Valve Gasket
7	Inlet Valve Seat
8	Inlet Valve
9	Inlet Valve Spring
10	Inlet Valve Stop
11	Unloader Piston Stop
12	Hex Head Screws
13	O-Ring
14	Inlet Strainer Gasket
15	Discharge Valve Stop
16	Discharge Valve Spring
17	Discharge Valve
18	Discharge Valve Seat
19	Cylinder Heat Gasket
20	Piston Ring Set (STD)
	#1 Piston Ring
	#2 Piston Ring
	Piston Ring Oil
	Expander Ring
21	Piston
	Wrist Pin Plug
	Wrist Pin
22	Connecting Rod
	Connecting Rod Cap
	Lockwasher
	Connecting Rod Bolt
23	O-ring
24	Thrust Washer
25	End Cover Assembly

5/16-In. Machine Screw With Lockwasher

NOTE: Some Applications Use Front And Rear Reference. Some Flange Mounts Without Bearings.

Single-cylinder compressor internal parts. *(Courtesy: Bendix Corp.)*

ture ring damage.

With the engine stopped, compressor air leakage can be detected by carefully listening at the compressor for the sound of escaping air.

Removal

NOTE: Most air compressors are rebuildable. However, if external leaks, knocking noises or blow-by are excessive, it may be prudent to replace the entire assembly.

Completely depressurize the air brake system and remove the belt (if equipped). The compressor-mounted governor, if equipped, is removed by loosening and removing the attaching screws, washers or nuts. After the governor is removed, discard the old gasket and clean all gasket material from the mating surfaces. If the compressor is water cooled, drain the coolant from the cylinder head. Before disconnecting air, water and oil lines to the compressor, inspect them for any signs of leakage. If leakage is found, replace the line(s) upon reassembly.

At this time, the compressor mounting bolts can be removed, and the compressor lifted from the engine compartment.

Disassembly

Much like an internal combustion engine, air compressors consist of cooling and lubricating systems, a cylinder head, pistons, cylinder block, crankshaft and crankcase.

Remove the compressor as previously outlined. On a workbench, remove the cylinder head bolts and gently tap the side of the cylinder head with a rubber mallet to break the gasket seal. Remove the head and gasket. Remove the inlet valves and guides from the compressor block taking care not to damage the valve seats. Unscrew the discharge cap nuts from the head and remove the discharge valves and springs. Clean all gasket material from the mating surfaces.

Remove the crankcase base plate. After the plate is removed, you can view the connecting rod caps from the bottom. Before removing the connecting rod bolts, mark each connecting rod and its bearing cap for assembly reference.

Some connecting rod bolts have locking tabs. If this is the case, bend the locking tab until there is sufficient room for the proper size wrench to fit onto the connecting rod bolt.

Remove the connecting rod bolts, washers and bearing caps. Push the connecting rods along with the pistons through the block. Be careful not to scratch the cylinder walls. Remove the pin retainers and press the pins out of the side of the piston using a suitable press. The connecting rods and rings can then be removed from the pistons.

Remove the cylinder block by loosening the block-to-crankcase bolts and separating the cylinder block from the crankcase.

If the crankshaft is belt driven, remove the crankshaft hub assembly. Remove the crankcase front and rear covers. Press the crankshaft and bearing out of the crankcase.

If the crankshaft is gear driven, remove the pin and nut from the front of the crankshaft. Remove the rear crankcase cover to expose the crank-

Compressor with gear-driven crankshaft.
(Courtesy: Bendix Commercial Vehicle Systems)

shaft and slide the crankshaft through the rear opening. Remove the front and rear thrust washers. Do not remove the crankshaft bearings, end cover or compressor gear unless you are planning to replace them.

Cleaning And Inspection

Clean all parts with a suitable cleaning solution and allow to dry thoroughly. Inspect parts for carbon deposits and clean if necessary. Clean all rust and scale from the cooling system and ensure that all passages are clear. Make sure all gasket material is removed from the mating surfaces.

CYLINDER HEAD

Inspect the cylinder head for cracks or damage and replace the head if any defects are found. Block all coolant ports except for one, and apply air pressure to the open coolant port. Check for leakage by applying soapy water to the outside of the head. The head should be replaced if leakage is found. Inspect the discharge valve seats for wear. If you find slight wear, the seats can be lapped using a lapping tool.

Check the discharge valves for leaks. Apply 100 psi of compressed air through the discharge port, and check the valve area with soapy water. As a general rule, leakage should not exceed 1-in. soap bubble every five seconds. (An alternative method is to monitor system pressure loss using the methods and specifications outlined by the vehicle-specific manufacturer. If excessive leakdown is found, use a soapy water solution or ultrasound detector to locate the leak source(s).) If you find unsuitable leakage, gently tap the discharge valves with a wood dowel to try to improve sealing. If the discharge valves are grooved, check the compressor manufacturer's specifications for groove tolerance and replace as necessary. When replacing discharge valves, seats or nuts,

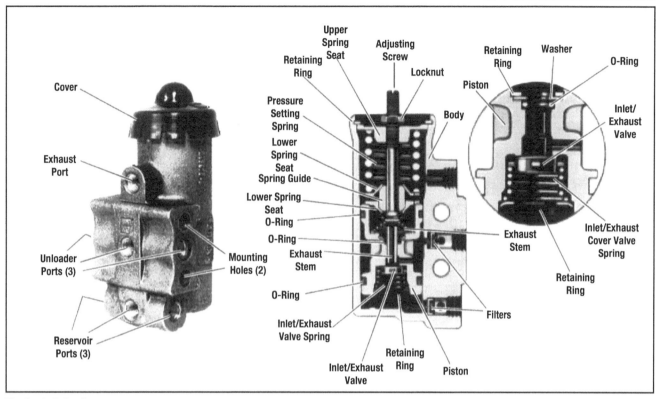

Typical air brake system governor. *(Courtesy: Bendix Corp.)*

check the valve travel according to the compressor manufacturer's instructions.

END COVERS

Check covers for cracks or damage and if the crankshaft main bearing is installed, check for excessive wear, looseness or flat spots. If any of these conditions exist, replace the end cover or bearing.

CYLINDER BLOCK

Visibly inspect the block for cracks. If cracks are found, the block must be replaced. Check the bore bushings for wear, rust or damage and replace in accordance with the compressor manufacturer's instructions. Inspect the inlet valve seats. If they show signs of wear, the seats can be lapped using a lapping tool. If they are excessively worn, they must be replaced. Inspect the inlet valves for grooves. Check the compressor manufacturer's specifications for allowable tolerances.

Using a micrometer, measure the cylinder bores. If the bores are scored

or out-of-round, they can be rebored or honed. Note that after the honing or reboring procedure, the cylinder bores should have a smooth, cross hatch finish just like an internal combustion engine. Next, clean the cylinder bores with hot, soapy water and a stiff brush. Wipe the bores with a clean cloth and motor oil. Finally, wipe the bores with a clean dry cloth until no dirt is present.

CONNECTING RODS/BEARINGS

Check connecting rod to pin clearance and ensure it's within manufacturer's specifications. Position the rod on the crank-shaft with the bearing insert installed. Install Plastigage® across the bearing insert in the cap. Install the cap and torque to about 11 ft-lbs. Remove the cap and check the clearance. If the clearance is not within specification, replace the bearings.

PISTONS AND RINGS

Inspect pistons for cracking or scores. Measure each piston with a micrometer in relation to its cylinder

bore. Check manufacturer's specifications for clearance. Using an inverted piston, install the piston ring into the cylinder about half-way through the ring travel. Check the ring end gap. Make sure it is within manufacturer's specifications. Install the rings onto the pistons, staggering the end gaps according to manufacturer's specifications.

CRANKSHAFT

Inspect keyways, threads, tapered ends and all surfaces for wear or damage. Inspect the journals for out-of-round. If the journal is out-of-round, the crank-shaft must be reground or replaced. Install the proper sized connecting rod bearing inserts. Inspect the main bearing journals for excessive wear. Examine the main bearings for wear or flat spots. If detected, replace the bearings. If the crankshaft is equipped with an oil seal ring grove, the crankshaft must not be worn so as not to obtain a good seal.

Make sure all the oil passages are open by running a wire through the passage if needed, and cleaning with a suitable solvent. If the compressor is gear-driven, inspect the rear cover, bearing and gear assembly.

Assembly

On compressors with belt-driven crankshafts, if equipped with a rear sleeve bearing, install the crankshaft bearing onto the crankshaft using a suitable press. Then, install the thrust bearing on the rear of the crankshaft with its grooves toward the front. Install the oil seal into the rear end cover groove, and install the rear end cover. Using a suitable press, install the crankshaft and front bearing. Then install the front cover, oil seal and new gasket.

If equipped with a rear ball bearing, install the oil seal rings onto the crankshaft. Position the crankshaft and bearings in the crankcase and carefully press the crankshaft and bearings into place. Replace end cap gaskets and seals. Install the end caps.

If the compressor has a gear-driven crankshaft, install the front cover using a new O-ring and gasket. Install the crank-shaft through the back of the crankcase, taking care not to damage it during installation. Install the rear cover using a new O-ring and gasket, making sure oil holes are aligned. Reinstall the pin and nut in the front of the crankshaft.

Using a new gasket, install the cylinder block onto the crankcase. Install and tighten bolts to manufacturer's specifications. Apply sufficient lubrication to the piston, rings, piston pin and connecting rods before assembly. Install the rings, staggering the ring gaps in accordance with manufacturer's recommendations. Insert the piston pin into the side of the piston and press through the rod assembly until there is sufficient clearance on both sides of the piston to install the retainers.

Install the proper size bearing insert into the bottom of the connecting rod. Using a suitable ring compressor, compress the rings and carefully lower the assembly through the cylinder bore from the top. Using a wood dowel, gently tap on the top of the piston the rest of the way until the rings are seated in the cylinder bore, slightly below the top.

NOTE: It is important to make sure the crankshaft journal is in the proper position to accept the connecting rod and its bearing insert.

Once the upper bearing is seated in the crankshaft journal, install the lower bearing, cap, bolts and locking tabs (if equipped). Torque the bolts to manufacturer's specifications and bend the locking tabs to secure the bolts.

Installation

If the compressor is belt driven, mount the compressor into the engine compartment and torque the mounting bolts to manufacturer's specifications. Reinstall all of the lines and if equipped, reinstall the governor with a new gasket. Replace the belt if necessary, inspect belt alignment and adjust to specifications.

If the compressor is gear-driven, the drive gear must be meshed with the timing gear on the engine prior to installation. A misaligned compressor drive gear can cause poor compressor air build up. On most engines, compressor timing is achieved by aligning the timing marks on the compressor drive gear and crankcase.

Bring the piston in the engine's No. 1 cylinder to Top Dead Center (TDC), and align the air compressor drive gear mark with the mark on the crankcase. After the marks are aligned, ensure the alignment mark on the crankcase is aligned with the coupling on the back of the compressor.

Start the engine and allow the air pressure to rise to its proper psi. Check the governor operation and make sure there are no leaks.

Governor

A defective or out of adjustment governor will cause the air compressor to function improperly. This will in turn lead to insufficient or excessive air build-up, poor stopping ability and compressor and valve damage.

The governor is designed to regulate the air compressor's output. The governor may be attached to the compressor or externally mounted in the engine compartment with a line connected to it from the compressor.

An air line from the supply reservoir is also connected to the governor. This line signals the governor that there is sufficient, or insufficient air pressure build-up in the reservoir. On a typical system, when the air pressure in the supply reservoir falls below 100 psi, the governor 'cuts in' and signals the compressor to deliver air to the primary reservoir.

When the system is full (around 125 psi), the governor 'cuts out' to shut off air delivery. On some trucks, air pressure build-up is controlled by an unloader valve, which signals the compressor to release air externally when the system is at its capacity. This system minimizes the amount of oil passed into the brake system since it discharges into the atmosphere.

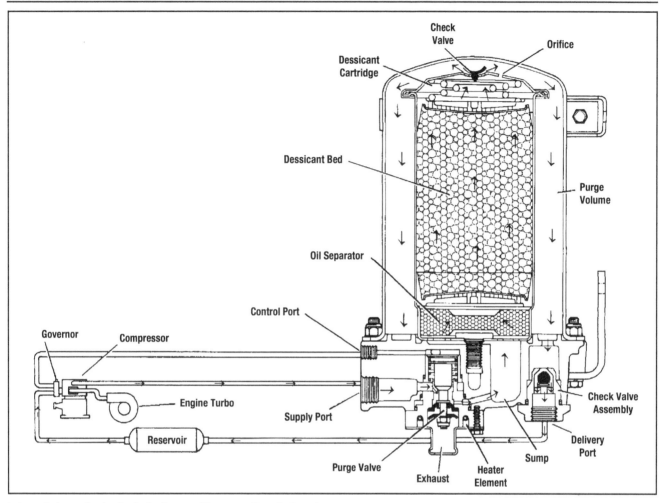

Internal view of a typical air dryer. *(Courtesy: Bendix Corp.)*

Diagnosis

To check the governor with the engine running, allow air pressure to build up in the system and observe at what pressure reading on the dash gauge the pressure stops climbing. This is the point of governor cut-out, which should be approximately 125 psi.

With the engine still running, slowly reduce the air pressure in the system by applying and releasing the brakes. Observe the pressure reading on the dash gauge at the point where the pressure starts to build up again. This is the point of governor cut-in, which should be approximately 100 psi.

Most governors are pre-set by the manufacturer. However, some are adjustable. If the governor does not cut the compressor in-and-out according to these specifications, either replace the assembly or adjust the governor pressure settings.

With the governor in the cut-out position, test for leakage at the exhaust valve by applying soap suds to the exhaust vent in the body. With the governor in the cut-in position, test for leakage of the inlet valve by applying soapy water to the exhaust vent in the body.

In either of these tests, leakage in excess of a 3-in. soap bubble in three seconds indicates the governor should be replaced. (See alternative test method information on page 14.)

Adjustment

NOTE: Before adjusting a governor, check the accuracy of the dash gauge with a test gauge. Also, take caution not to over-adjust the governor. Each 1/4 turn of the adjustment screw can raise or lower the pressure settings

approximately 4 psi.

Do not attempt to adjust a governor if its cover is marked non-adjustable and the adjustment screw is sheared off. If an adjustment screw is present, remove the top cover of the governor and loosen the screw locknut. To raise the pressure setting, turn the adjustment screw counterclockwise. To lower the setting, turn the screw clockwise. After verifying the correct pressures, tighten the locknut and install the governor top cover.

Removal And Installation

Completely depressurize the air brake system. Disconnect the air line(s). Remove the governor mounting bolts and the governor. If the governor is compressor mounted, clean all gasket material from the mating surfaces. Clean all ports and line inlets/outlets. Install the governor assembly using a new gasket.

If the governor is mounted elsewhere in the engine compartment, it should be mounted in a position higher than the compressor, and with the exhaust port facing downwards to allow for drainage away from the governor. Clean and reconnect all governor lines. Start the engine and check for leaks and proper operation.

Air Hoses And Lines

Air hose and line leakage will lead to poor stopping ability. In addition, a misrouted or malfunctioning hose or line can cause premature wear, pulling, grabbing or dragging.

Air hoses and lines carry compressed air from the air tanks to the valves and brake chambers. Air lines are made of either copper or stiff nylon, and are used in areas where no movement is required. Air hoses are made of rubber, and are designed to move with the truck's suspension, steering, and areas where movement is present. Hoses are comprised of layers of synthetic rubber, allowing the hose to be strong but retain its flexibility.

Inspection

Most brake manufacturers recommend that a visual inspection for chafed or badly routed lines and hoses and other obvious wear and damage be made whenever any brake service is required. However, it is also recommended that the driver perform a daily visual inspection.

Of course, an air leak is the main reason to replace a line or a hose. However, there are other telltale signs that a hose should be replaced. Hoses and lines should be replaced if bulging or swelling is apparent when the brakes are fully applied. Also, improper routing, clamping and crimping are cause for replacement.

Replacement

Completely depressurize the air

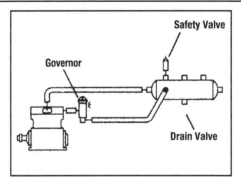

The reservoir safety valve protects the air brake system against excessive air built-up.
(Courtesy: Bendix Commercial Vehicle Systems)

brake system. It is not recommended, and in most cases illegal, to splice or patch a leaking brake line or hose. Hoses must be replaced with DOT approved material intended for the specific application. Also, do not change the diameter of a hose or line. It is important to properly route a hose or line to avoid bending, kinking and wear-through problems. Finally, use the correct ferrules, inserts and nuts when replacing a hose or line.

Reservoir Safety Valve

A defective reservoir safety valve will cause excessive air pressure build up in the brake system leading to accelerated valve wear, premature brake wear, pulling, grabbing and dragging.

The reservoir safety valve, also called a pop off or air tank relief valve, is a normally closed valve designed to ensure that the primary air reservoir is not over pressurized. The valve consists of a spring-loaded ball assembly. When air pressure in the reservoir rises to an above normal state, the spring-loaded ball is unseated, allowing system air to vent to the atmosphere through the valve. As air pressure returns to normal, spring tension forces the ball to seat, closing the valve.

To determine if the air pressure safety valve is operative, pull the exposed end of the valve stem. If

the safety valve does not blow off when the stem is pulled, the valve ball is probably stuck in its seat. Check the valve area with soapy water. As a general rule, leakage should not exceed 1-in. soap bubble every five seconds.

The reservoir safety valve is replaced by completely depressurizing the air brake system and unscrewing the valve from the reservoir.

Reservoir Drain Valves

A defective reservoir drain valve will allow moisture and other contaminates to work their way into the brake system, leading to poor stopping ability and valve wear.

Manual or automatic drain valves are installed in each reservoir to help purge the system. Manual valves should be drained on a daily basis, especially in humid or wet climates where excessive amounts of moisture is present.

Automatic drain valves are designed to expel moisture and contaminants from the reservoir without the aid of manual operation. When the governor cut-out pressure is reached and the reservoir pressure begins to drop, the valve opens, allowing moisture and con-

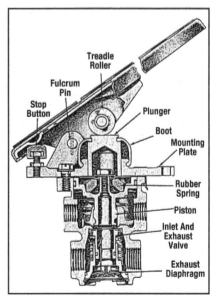

Internal view of a brake foot (or application) valve.

taminants to be ejected from the reservoir.

Fully pressurize the air brake system. Check the drain valve using soapy water. There should be no leaks at the drain valve exhaust port or at the threads where the valve screws into the reservoir. If leaks are found, replace the valve by completely depressurizing the air brake system, and unscrewing the valve from the reservoir.

Air Dryers

A defective air dryer will allow moisture and other contaminants into the brake system, leading to poor stopping ability and valve wear.

Most air brake systems use an air dryer, which contains desiccant material to keep condensation out of the supply reservoir. Air passes through the desiccant, and moisture is absorbed into the material. When a system is equipped with an air dryer, daily reservoir draining is not recommended unless extreme conditions exist.

The air dryer's main function is to remove moisture and contaminants from the air system before the compressed air travels to the primary reservoir. The air dryer operates in two cycles, charge and purge.

The charge cycle accepts compressed air sometimes contaminated with moisture or debris from the air compressor. Compressed air travels through an oil separator where oil and solid contaminants are removed. Water and water vapor are removed from the air by way of desiccant material. The air then enters the primary tank through a one-way check valve. Once the governor cut-out pressure is achieved, the governor signals the air dryer to begin the purge cycle.

This signal opens the purge port of the air dryer to allow contaminants to exit through to the atmosphere. The valve stays open until the governor cut-in pressure is achieved, signaling the compressor to once again build air pressure.

Diagnosis

To test the outlet port check valve, completely depressurize the air brake system. Install a pressure gauge in the primary reservoir, and build up air pressure to governor cut-out pressure. A rapid loss of air could indicate a problem with the air dryer outlet port check valve. To confirm this, completely depressurize the air brake system again, and remove the check valve from the end cover. Apply air pressure to the unit and apply soapy water to the check valve side. Leakage should not exceed a 1-in. soap bubble in one second. (See alternative test method information on page 14.)

To test the purge valve, build up pressure in the system. With the compressor operating, apply soapy water to the purge valve housing exhaust port. Leakage should not exceed a 1-in. soap bubble in one second.

Close all reservoir drain valves and build the air brake system until the governor cuts-out. Listen to the air dryer purge valve to see if air is purged at governor cut-out. Reduce the system air pressure until the governor cuts in and repeat the procedure.

Air Dryer Heater

Check the heater by moving the ignition switch to the ON position (key on engine off). Unplug the air dryer connection, and check for voltage to the dryer. If there is no voltage, check for a blown fuse, broken wire or wire corrosion. Also, inspect the system for a good ground.

If specified voltage is present, check the heater and thermostat operation. To do this, move the ignition switch to the OFF position and cool the end cover to a temperature below 40 degrees. Check the resistance between the dryer connector and the electrical pins. If resistance is higher then the manufacturer's specifications, replace the thermostat and heater assembly.

Next, heat the end cover to a temperature above 90 degrees and check resistance again according to manu-facturer's specifications. If resistance is higher then the manufacturer's specifications, replace the thermostat and heater assembly.

To replace the air dryer, completely depressurize the air brake system. Mark and disconnect all air lines. Unplug wire connections. Loosen the upper air dryer mounting strap. Mark and remove the end cover nuts, screws and washers. Remove the air dryer assembly.

The heater and thermostat on most air dryers is housed in the purge valve housing assembly. If the heater and/or thermostat are proven defective, replace the entire purge valve housing assembly.

PURGE VALVE HOUSING

Remove the delivery check valve and its O-ring. Remove the purge valve housing screws and the valve housing (containing the heater and thermostat) from the end cover. Remove the O-rings from the housing and the bore.

Lubricate all new O-rings and sealing surfaces with a suitable lubricant prior to assembly. Install the purge valve housing with new O-rings, and install the housing onto the end cover. Install the delivery check valve along with a new O-ring.

SERVICE SYSTEM

Pneumatic imbalance is the improper delivery of air pressure to the service brake chambers. The most common causes are improperly functioning relay, check or safety valves, air leaks, restricted air lines, a defective foot valve, pressure limiting valve, spring brake valve, push-pull valve, or a quick-release valve not exhausting properly.

Dragging brakes or improper trailer braking can be the result of a defective tractor protection valve, air leaks, restricted air lines, a defective foot valve, spring brake valve, push-pull valve, trailer control valve, or a quick-release valve not

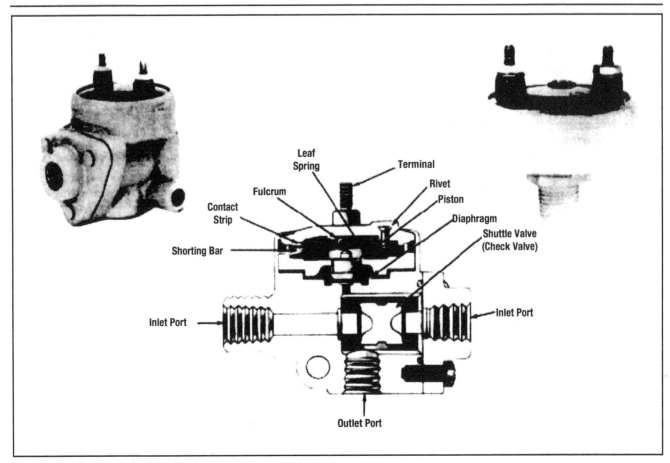

Stoplight switch and double check valve. *(Courtesy: Bendix Corp.)*

exhausting properly.

Federal regulations require that air brake systems on trucks manufactured after 1975 be of the 'split' service system. Split air systems consist of a primary and secondary circuit so that in the event of a failure, one portion of the brake system can allow the driver to bring the truck to a controlled stop.

The primary circuit controls the brakes at the rear wheels, while the secondary circuit controls the brakes at the front. Check valves are used to keep the systems separate, thus preventing air loss in both circuits in the event that one fails. It must be noted that this system is only meant to enable the driver to safely stop the truck in the event of a malfunction. Since the compressed air will follow the path of least resistance, the system will only perform until the accumulated air is depleted.

The split service system consists of a series of pneumatic valves that direct air and control pressure to appropriate components.

Foot Valve

Insufficient stopping power, improper brake release, grabbing, pulling and drag can be the result of a defective foot (or application) valve.

Foot valves may be either floor or bulkhead mounted. As a rule of thumb, foot valves are designed to maintain pressure in the 5-80 psi range, as well as applying full pressure when fully applied. It is called a dual-control foot valve, because it is actually two valves that operate simultaneously in response to input from the driver's foot at the brake pedal. Two valves are necessary because it controls both the primary and secondary parts of the split service system.

Diagnosis

An ultrasonic leak detector can be used at the exhaust port to detect internal air leaks. The tool transposes the sound of an air leak, no matter how small, into a frequency that can be heard through headphones. Also, the intensity of the signal can be observed on an LCD display. In all other cases, soapy water can be used.

As a general rule, foot control valves are replaced as an assembly. However, a seal kit and maintenance kit is available for most models. Consult the manufacturer's recommendations before attempting to overhaul the unit.

EXHAUST PORT

Start the engine and allow the air pressure to build to its proper pressure. Stop the engine.

With the foot pedal fully released, coat the foot valve exhaust port with soapy water to check for leaks.

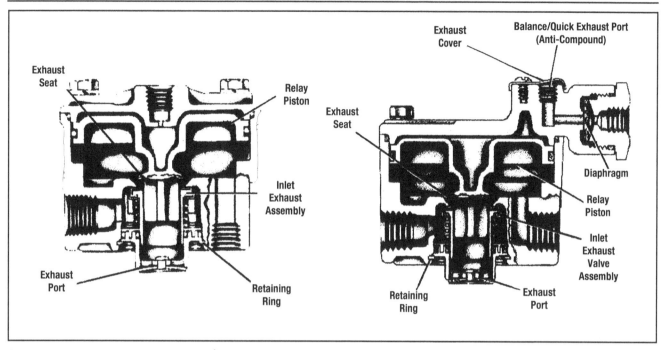

Sectional view of two types of relay valves. *(Courtesy: Bendix Corp.)*

Next, have an assistant fully apply the foot pedal. Coat the exhaust port again with soapy water and check for leaks. Leaks causing less than a 3-in. soap bubble in 3 seconds are permissible. (See alternative test method information on page 14.)

PRIMARY AND SECONDARY PORTS

Completely depressurize the air brake system and connect suitable air brake system pressure gauges to the primary and secondary discharge ports. Start the engine and allow air to build up to the governed pressure. Have an assistant depress the brake pedal while you note the gauge readings at several positions between fully released, and fully depressed.

The air pressure should increase in proportion to the brake pedal travel. Also, primary and secondary pressures should be within 5 psi of each other. With the pedal still depressed, note the difference between the primary and secondary readings and the dash gauge. They should not differ more than 5 psi. If

the foot valve fails any one of these tests, it should be replaced.

Foot Valve Removal

Inspect the foot valve and its bracket closely. Some valves can be removed with the bracket intact. Completely depressurize the system. Mark and disconnect all supply and delivery lines. Mark and remove any electrical connections. Remove the foot valve mounting bolts and the brake pedal (if necessary), and remove the valve.

Cleaning And Inspection

On most models, the inlet-exhaust poppet valve can be inspected by removing the retaining ring and shield located in the exhaust port at the bottom of the valve. Guide seal friction tends to hold the parts assembled; however, the spring will gradually force the parts out.

The reaction piston can be inspected by removing the spring retainer from the top of the valve body. Separate the body from the mounting flange. Pull the treadle fulcrum pin and lift off the treadle (if equipped) in order to reach one mounting screw.

Should the operation of the valve become slow or hesitant after prolonged service, disassemble and clean the unit. When re-assembling the valve, cover all bearing surfaces with a thin film of suitable lubrication.

Installation

Install the brake pedal and mounting bracket (if necessary). Install the foot valve and its mounting bolts. Reconnect all supply, delivery and electrical connections. Start the engine and allow air pressure to build to its proper pressure. Check the valve for leaks and proper operation.

Maintenance

Follow the manufacturer's maintenance schedules for the following:
- Check the brake pedal and linkage for proper operation
- Lubricate all moving linkage components
- Make sure all ports are clean and free of debris
- Disassemble and replace seals.

Stoplight Switch

The stoplight switch is an electro-pneumatic, non-grounded switch

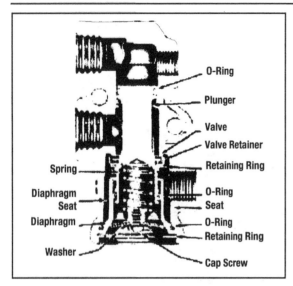

Sectional view of a tractor protection valve. *(Courtesy: Bendix Corp.)*

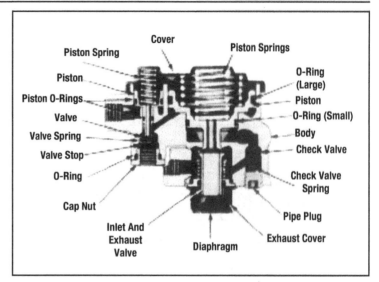

Sectional view of a typical spring brake valve. *(Courtesy: Bendix Corp.)*

that operates in tandem with a two-way check valve. When the brakes are applied, the air pressure moves an internal switch that completes the circuit, activating the stoplights.

Check for voltage at the electrical connection. If there is no voltage, check the fuse and wiring. If voltage is present, install an air gauge in the service line and gradually apply the brakes. The stoplights should illuminate at 6 psi or less. Check for air leaks at the switch. No air leaks are permissible.

Trailor Control Valve

A defective or leaking trailer control valve will not allow application of the trailer parking brakes independent of the tractor parking brakes.

The trailer control valve is a hand valve mounted in the cab. Its primary function is to allow the operator to check the fifth wheel connection integrity by attempting to move the coupled vehicle with the trailer brakes applied.

Because of its graduated application, some drivers use the trailer control valve by applying it while the combination is in motion to save wear and tear on the tractor brakes. This practice is not recommended. In some cases it can be hazardous,

causing trailer sway while driving, and increasing wear of the trailer brakes.

By rotating the lever counterclockwise, the valve allows reservoir air pressure to flow out to the trailer. By rotating the lever clockwise, the exhaust passage will open, allowing air pressure to the trailer brakes to exhaust.

Diagnosis

Completely depressurize the air brake system. Connect an air pressure gauge to the delivery port and charge the system until the governor cuts-out. Fully apply the valve and read the pressure gauge. The gauge pressure should equal system pressure. There should be no leakage at the exhaust port of the valve.

Fully release the valve and observe that air pressure escapes from the exhaust port. At this time, the gauge pressure should read zero. There should be no leakage at the exhaust port of the valve. Slowly apply the valve and notate the pressure readings. The readings should progressively rise and fall with the valve application/release.

Removal

Completely depressurize the air brake system. Remove the handle

assembly and dash panel (if applicable) to gain access to the valve. Mark and disconnect the air lines, and remove the mounting bolts and the valve.

Disassembly

Remove the handle O-ring, set-screw and head seal O-ring. Remove the adjusting ring lock washer, head seal O-ring and head. Separate the valve cover from the body. Remove the gasket and graduating spring. Remove the cam and cam follower from the cover. Remove the adjusting ring, piston, piston return spring and piston O-ring. Remove the exhaust and inlet valves and their O-rings.

Cleaning and Inspection

Clean all metal parts in a suitable solution. Inspect the valves and seats for damage. Inspect the valve body and springs for damage or corrosion.

Assembly

Install the inlet and exhaust valves with new O-rings. Install the piston with a new O-ring into the valve body. Install the adjusting ring lock washer, head seal O-ring and head. Install the cam follower and cam into the cover assembly. Install the gradu-

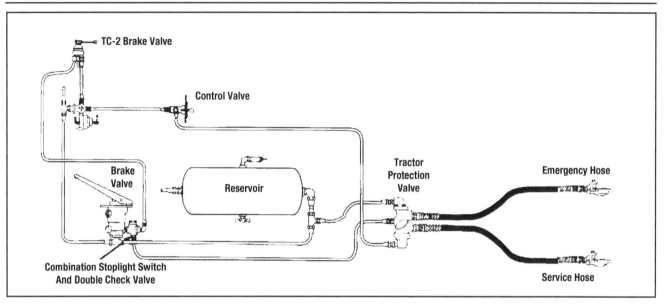

Trailer control valve and air piping. *(Courtesy: Bendix Corp.)*

ating spring into the valve body. Install the handle O-ring, setscrew and handle assembly.

Installation

Install the valve assembly to the mounting. Install the handle assembly. Start the engine and pressurize the system until the governor cuts-out. Check for leaks and proper operation. Install the dash panel (if applicable).

Relay Valves

A defective relay valve can cause premature brake wear, pulling, grabbing or dragging.

Relay valves are used on trailers and on the rear axles of long-wheel-based tractors to minimize delay of brake application due to length of plumbing. These valves are directly supplied with unmodulated air pressure, and use air from the dual-control foot valve or manual trailer valve as a signal to quickly direct air to the brakes they serve.

Relay valves come in a variety of 'crack' pressures. Crack pressure is the air pressure value required at the input from the foot valve before the relay valve will send air pressure to the brakes controlled by that valve. Crack pressure is an important element of brake timing and balance and is de-

termined, axle-by-axle, by:

- how heavily loaded the axle served by a valve is
- the size of the axle's brakes
- how aggressive the linings are on those brakes.

A valve that cracks at pressure too low for a given axle can cause premature application, wheel lock-up and trailer pushing, if the affected axle is on the tractor. A valve that cracks at pressure too high for a given axle can cause delayed application, insufficient braking and trailer pushing, if the affected axle is on the trailer.

Diagnosis

Make sure the air brake system is fully pressurized. Apply the brakes several times and check for prompt operation at each wheel.

NOTE: Check the manufacturer's recommendations to find out if these checks are to be made with the parking brakes released or applied.

Apply soapy water to the exhaust port and the retaining ring. Leakage permitted is equal to a 1-in. soap bubble in three seconds. (See alternative test method information on page 14.) Apply soapy water to the valve body area. There should be no leakage.

Disassembly

Most relay valves are of the 'piston' type. Disassembly consists of removing the cover, relay piston, inlet/exhaust assembly, retaining rings, O-rings and diaphragm (if equipped). Consult the valve manufacturer for specific overhaul procedures.

Quick Release Valve

A defective quick release valve can cause slow brake release and premature brake wear, grabbing or dragging.

After a stop, when the driver lifts his foot from the brake pedal, a quick release valve allows brake actuation air to be quickly exhausted near the brakes it serves, rather than having to travel back through the supply line, thus speeding brake release time.

Diagnosis

The minimum apply and release times required by Federal Motor Truck Safety Standards are 0.45 seconds (apply time) and 0.55 seconds (release time) for tractors and straight trucks, and 0.6 seconds (apply time) and 1.2 seconds (release time) for non-pulling (single) trailers.

Disassembly

Remove the valve cover. Remove the spring and spring seat (if

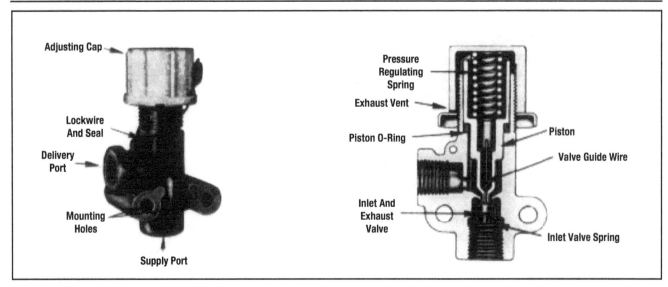

Pressure limiting valve and its internal components. *(Courtesy: Bendix Corp.)*

equipped). Remove the diaphragm O-ring.

Cleaning And Inspection

Clean all removed parts in a suitable cleaning solution. Inspect the diaphragm closely for any damage. Check the exhaust seat for damage. Check the spring seat for wear (if equipped).

Assembly

Install the valve seat and spring (if equipped). Install the diaphragm and O-ring. Install the valve cover.

Tractor Protection Valve

A defective tractor protection valve can send insufficient air pressure to the trailer causing premature brake wear, grabbing or dragging.

A tractor protection valve senses pressure in one or both lines that carry air to the trailer. These lines are connected to the trailer by means of quick-connect air fittings called 'gladhands.' When there is no pressure in the line(s) due to trailer breakaway or a gross air leak in the trailer circuit, the valve closes to maintain air pressure in the tractor circuit.

In everyday use, the valve also works in conjunction with the dash-mounted trailer parking brake valve to shut off air to the trailer circuit before disconnecting the tractor from the trailer.

Diagnosis

Pressurize the air brake system to 100 psi. Have an assistant fully apply the brakes. Using soapy water, check for leakage at the disconnected couplings. Leak-age should not exceed 1-in. soap bubble in five seconds. Connect the trailer supply line and supply air to the trailer via the supply valve. Leakage at the supply line should not exceed 1-in. bubble in five seconds. (See alternative test method information on page 14.)

Removal And Installation

Completely depressurize the air brake system. Remove the trailer hoses leading from the valve. Mark and disconnect the tractor service and supply lines, then remove the valve.

Install the valve assembly onto its mounting. Reconnect the tractor service and supply lines. Reconnect the trailer hoses. Start the engine and allow air pressure to build to its proper pressure. Check the valve for leaks and proper operation.

Spring Brake Valve

A defective spring brake valve will allow the parking brakes to apply themselves in the event of a leak, causing premature brake wear, grab-bing or dragging.

The spring brake (or multi-function) valve limits the air pressure used to keep the trailer parking brakes off. By means of an integral check-valve, this valve also isolates a failed reservoir, which would otherwise cause the parking brakes to be automatically applied.

Diagnosis

FUNCTIONALITY CHECK

Pressurize the air brake system until governor cut-out is achieved. Engage the dash mounted parking brake control valve, making sure that the spring brakes apply promptly and hold sufficiently. Per Federal Motor Vehicle Safety Standards, the parking brakes must be able to hold a vehicle, loaded to its gross weight rating, stationary on a smooth, dry, concrete roadway facing uphill or downhill on a 20% grade.

Release the parking brake control valve and make sure that the spring brakes release promptly. Note the dash pressure and replace the valve if not within manufacturer's specifications.

Engage the dash mounted parking brake control valve again and observe the gauge reading. It should drop to zero. Release the parking brake control valve and completely drain the air from the primary reservoir. Press the brake pedal several times while making sure the pressure gauge reading decreases each time. After several applications the spring brakes will no longer actuate.

LEAKAGE CHECK

Fully pressurize the air brake system and release the parking brake control valve. Coat the valve and exhaust port with soapy water. Slight leakage is permitted.

The valve can be replaced by completely depressurizing the air brake system, marking and removing the air lines and removing the valve from its mounting.

Two-Way Check Valve

A defective two-way check valve can cause poor stopping, premature wear, brake noise, pulling, grabbing and dragging.

The two-way check-valve senses primary and secondary supply pressure and allows the dominant pressure to actuate the trailer brakes. Primary air can also be manually supplied to the trailer by means of a hand valve, usually located on or near the steering column.

Two-way check-valves are also used to allow dominant pressure to activate the stop light switch,

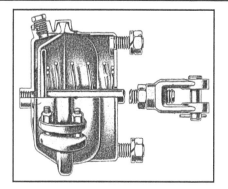

Brake chamber.

and to release the parking brakes. Federal Motor Vehicle Safety Standards (FMVSS) require that the driver be able to release the parking brakes at least once from the cab in the event of a failure in either circuit.

Diagnosis

Pump the brake pedal to see if the brakes apply and release on both the tractor and trailer. Engage the trailer supply dash valve and make sure that the trailer brakes apply and release. Apply the trailer brakes by engaging the trailer supply dash valve. Check the exhaust port of the foot valve for leakage with soapy water. Leakage of 1-in. soap bubble in five seconds is permissible. (See alternative test method

information on page 14.)

Have an assistant apply and hold the brake pedal. Check the exhaust port of the trailer supply valve for leakage with soapy water. Leakage of 1-in. soap bubble in 5 seconds is permissible. (See alternative test method information on page 14.)

Install a pressure gauge in the outlet port. Apply and release air to one inlet port and observe that the gauge registers application and release.

To replace the valve, completely depressurize the air brake system, disconnect the air lines and remove the valve from its mounting. After replacing the valve, start the engine and build up pressure until the governor cuts-out. Check for leaks and proper operation.

Pressure Limiting Valve

A defective pressure limiting valve can over-pressurize systems not needing full brake pressure, causing damage to system components.

The pressure limiting (or proportioning) valve reduces pressure to air brake components that do not necessarily need full system pressure such as air suspensions, tank vents and drains.

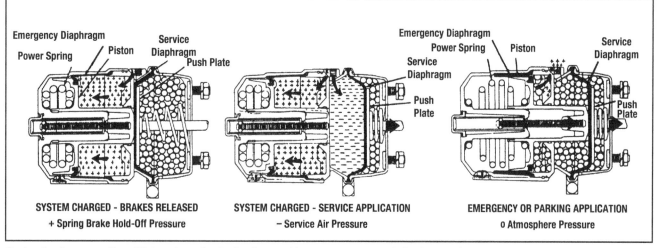

Spring brake operation. Piston-type brake is shown. However, a second diaphragm is often used in place of the piston. In normal mode, system pressure overcomes spring pressure, and the parking brake is held off. During normal service brake application, service air acts on a diaphragm in the right chamber, and is not affected by the spring brake. In emergency or parking operation, air is exhausted from the left chamber. Spring force moves the pushrod to the right, applying the parking brake.

Diagnosis

Run the engine and build up air pressure until the governor cuts-out. Apply soapy water around the valve cap. Leakage should be no more than 1-in. soap bubble in three seconds. (See alternative test method information on page 14.)

Drain the air pressure from the delivery side and disconnect the air line. Apply soapy water to the delivery port. Leakage should be no more than 1-in. soap bubble in five seconds. (See alternative test method information on page 14.)

Connect an air pressure gauge to the delivery line of the valve and inspect its closing pressure. If the air pressure varies more than 5 psi from sthe valve setting, either replace the valve, or adjust it (if applicable) by turning the adjustment cap.

Run the engine and pressurize the system. Observe the inlet valve opening pressure. If it is more than 5 psi from the valve pressure setting, adjust or replace the valve. The valve is replaced by completely depressurizing the air brake system, marking and removing the lines, and removing the valve from its mounting.

MECHANICAL/ FOUNDATION AND WHEEL BEARINGS

If the vehicle's brakes are pulling to one side, grabbing too quickly, improperly releasing, or otherwise causing the vehicle to experience poor stopping ability, the system could be experiencing what is called 'mechanical imbalance.'

When checking mechanical imbalance, the first thing to look for is improperly adjusted brakes. Brakes that are out of adjustment often display symptoms of more complex problems, especially when all the brakes are not adjusted to the same degree. This results in brake imbalance and increased stopping distance.

Moreover, the remaining properly adjusted brakes are forced to do extra work, resulting in excessive heat and wear. While a heat-damaged drum and prematurely worn lining at one or more wheel ends could indicate a dragging brake, make sure you check for an out-of-adjustment condition at all wheel ends.

If the brakes are improperly adjusted, make sure the slack adjusters are working properly and all adjusters are free. Make sure the brake chamber rod is not bent. Then, adjust the brakes.

If the brakes are found to be adjusted properly, look for inoperative brake chambers, worn brake hardware, cracked brake spiders, worn, tapered, glazed or cracked brake shoes, drums with scoring, cracking, excessive inner diameter and/or runout, and sticking wheel cylinder or caliper pistons. Also, make sure the brake adjusters, air chamber brackets, anchor pins and cam rollers are lubricated as per the manufacturer's recommendations.

Lubrication is an oft-forgotten PM measure. Whenever a truck is brought in for chassis lubrication, brake adjusters, air chamber brackets, anchor pins and cam rollers should be lubed, too. This helps automatic brake adjusters stay automatic, keeps manual adjusters easily adjustable, allows camshafts to rotate freely, and staves off costly wear. Follow manufacturers' lubrication recommendations, and avoid getting grease or oil on brake linings.

Service Brake Chamber

A defective service brake chamber will cause severe brake balance problems, contributing to premature brake wear at other wheel positions, pulling to one side, and overall poor stopping ability of the vehicle.

When the brake pedal is depressed, air pressure is directed to brake chambers at each wheel end. Each brake chamber consists of a pressure housing, a diaphragm, and a pushrod. As air pressure is exerted on the diaphragm, the pushrod on the other side of the diaphragm is extended, activating the brakes.

The force exerted by the pushrod is the product of the amount of air pressure applied in psi, and the area of the diaphragm in square inches. For example, 60 psi applied to a chamber with a 16-square-in. diaphragm would create a force at the pushrod of 960 lbs. A 60-psi application to a chamber with a 30-square-inch diaphragm would yield 1800 lbs. of pushrod force. Obviously, improperly matched brake chambers can cause severe brake balance problems.

Diagnosis

FUNCTIONALITY CHECK

Check that mounting brackets are secure and damage free. Apply and release the brakes to make sure pushrods operate freely. Inspect for proper pushrod travel, making sure that the travel is as short as possible without the brakes dragging.

LEAKAGE CHECK

While holding the brake pedal down, apply soapy water to the clamp and the line inlet. No leakage is permissible. If leakage is detected, try to tighten the clamp. Be careful not to over tighten the clamp.

Removal

WARNING: If the service brake chamber is equipped with a spring brake, follow the manufacturer's recommendations for caging the unit before servicing. Failure to do so can lead to serious injury.

Completely depressurize the air brake system and disconnect the air line from the brake chamber. Remove the yoke pin and the brake chamber from its bracket.

Disassembly

The chamber is disassembled by pulling out the pushrod and clamping it at the non-pressure plate. Remove the clamp nuts and bolts, and spread the ring slightly to remove the clamp from the plate. Do not damage or distort the clamp. Remove the pressure plate and chamber diaphragm. Remove the yoke from the pushrod and release the grip on the rod, being careful to contain the assembly until the return spring is relaxed. Remove the pushrod, spring and boot or O-ring (if equipped).

Assembly

Stand the pushrod upright on a flat surface and position the return spring on the rod. Install the boot or O-ring (if equipped) on the non-pressure plate. Position the plate onto the pushrod and press it down against spring tension until it bottoms out. Clamp the rod.

Position the clamping ring over the surface of the non-pressure plate. Install the diaphragm in the pressure plate and install onto the non-pressure plate. Work the ring clamp over the clamping surface of the pressure plate and tighten with a suitable tool. Install the clamp bolt and nut and tighten. Release the grip on the pushrod and install the bolt and nut.

Installation

Mount the brake chamber onto its bracket. Install the yoke and yoke pin. Check the angle of the pushrod and slack adjuster. The angle should be greater than 90 degrees in the released position. Connect the brake line and make sure that it is properly routed.

Automatic Slack Adjuster

The automatic slack adjuster is essentially a lever that multiplies force in proportion to its length in order to keep brakes adjusted. Automatic slack adjusters should never be manually adjusted except for an initial adjustment after installation and adjustment to enable a vehicle for transport after a malfunction. A properly

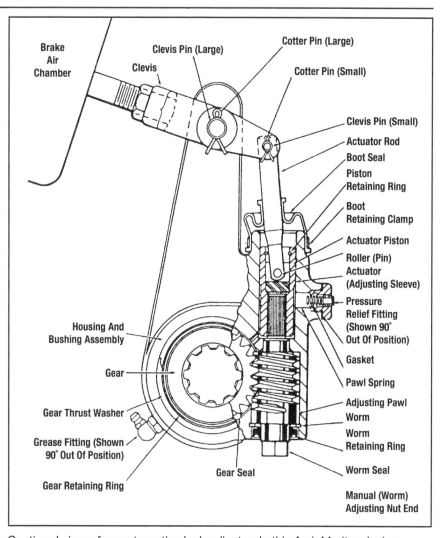

Sectional view of an automatic slack adjuster. In this ArvinMeritor design, chamber pushrod extension pulls the actuator rod and turns the adjuster worm screw. *(Courtesy: ArvinMeritor Corp.)*

trained technician should only perform adjustments after replacement of the slack adjuster.

According to the National Transportation Board (NTSB) recommendations:

Manually adjusting automatic slack adjusters is dangerous and should not be done, except during installation or in an emergency to move the vehicle to a repair facility, because manual adjustment of this brake component:
1. Fails to address the true reason why the brakes are not maintaining adjustment, giving *the operator a false sense of security about the effectiveness of the brakes, which are likely to go out of adjustment again soon.*
2. Causes abnormal wear to the internal adjusting mechanism for most automatic slack adjusters, which may lead to failure of this brake component.

It is crucial to understand that out-of-adjustment brakes equipped with automatic slack adjusters are most likely exhibiting some other failure symptom that cannot be solely remedied by adjustments.

Automatic slack adjusters come in two variations; stroke sensing and clearance sensing. Stroke sensing slack adjusters are designed to react to the amount of brake chamber push rod travel. If the travel is past a pre-determined limit, the unit will adjust the brakes accordingly. Clearance sensing slack adjusters are designed to sense the lining-to-drum clearance and adjust when the brakes are released.

A defective slack adjuster will fail to compensate for brake lining wear and contribute to premature brake wear at the other wheel positions, pulling to one side, and overall poor stopping ability.

Diagnosis

When checking automatic slack adjusters, inspect the free stroke, which is the amount of adjuster arm movement required to seat the brake shoes against the drum. Always use the adjuster manufacturer's specific procedures and specifications.

Next, check the brake-applied stroke. This is the measurement of slack adjuster arm movement from a fully retracted position to a brake applied position at manufacturer's PSI recommendations.

If the free stroke is within manufacturer's specifications, but the applied stroke is not, suspect a problem with the foundation brakes. If both the free stroke and applied stroke are out of specification, suspect either a foundation brake or automatic slack adjuster problem.

If the foundation brakes are intact and operating properly, inspect the automatic slack adjuster operation in strict accordance with the manufacturer's recommended procedures. Most manufacturers recommend checking the slack adjuster internal clutch using a torque wrench.

Place the torque wrench on the adjusting hex and turn the wrench counter-clockwise. When a ratcheting sound is heard, record the torque and compare with manufacturer's specifications. If the clutch ratchets at a

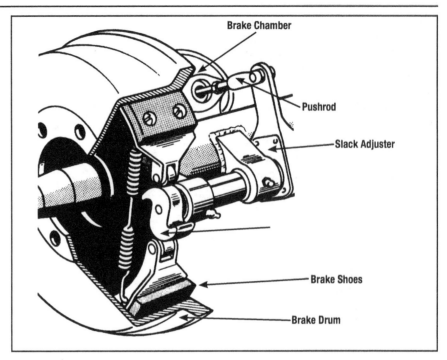

When the pushrod is extended, the brake adjuster, camshaft and S-cam rotate. The S-cam spreads the brake shoes apart and against the brake drum. *(Courtesy: ArvinMeritor Corp.)*

lower than specified torque, replace the slack adjuster.

Removal

WARNING: Consult the manufacturer's recommendations when replacing a slack adjuster. If the service brake chamber is equipped with a spring brake, follow the manufacturer's recommendations for caging the unit before servicing. Failure to do so can lead to serious injury.

Disconnect the brake chamber pushrod and yoke from the slack adjuster. Remove the retainer from the brake camshaft. Rotate the slack adjuster and slide the slack adjuster from the brake camshaft.

Installation

Clean the brake camshaft splines and coat the splines and brake chamber push rod with anti-seize compound. Mount the slack adjuster onto the brake camshaft and install the retainer per manufacturer's speci-

fications. Install the brake chamber pushrod and yoke. On initial installation, it may be necessary to remove the self-adjusting pawl before the slack can be manually adjusted. Adjust the mechanism until the brake lining makes contact with the drum. Back off the adjuster in accordance with manufacturer's specifications. Measure free stroke and applied stroke again.

Cam Type Brakes

Worn anchor pins, mounting holes, bushings or outer S-cam bushings can allow applied force to push the shoes to one side, resulting in tapered lining wear. This condition often is accompanied by outer edge abrasion on the brake shoes. The shoes track out of alignment and therefore scrape against the drum. Reusing shoe rollers and anchor pins, therefore, is not recommended.

Most air systems employ S-cam foundation brakes, so named because an S-shaped cam rotates to force the brake shoes and linings against

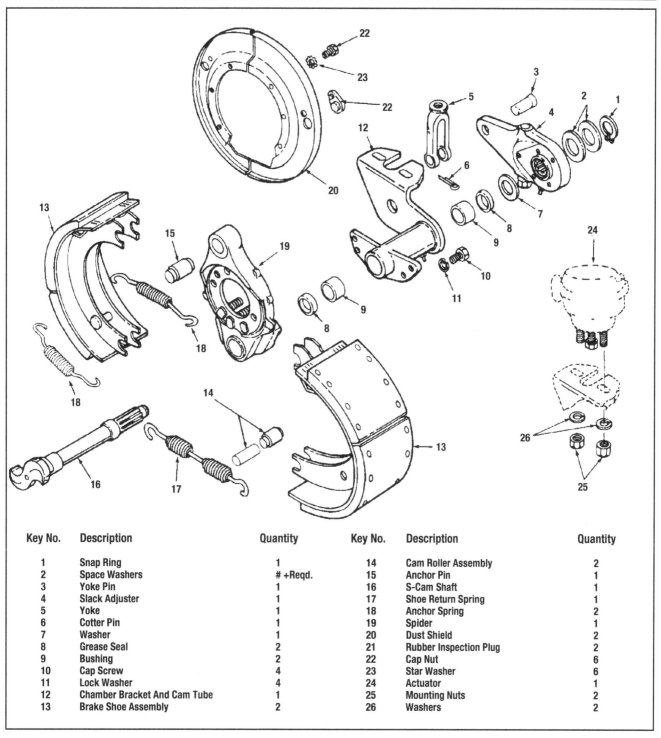

Key No.	Description	Quantity	Key No.	Description	Quantity
1	Snap Ring	1	14	Cam Roller Assembly	2
2	Space Washers	# +Reqd.	15	Anchor Pin	1
3	Yoke Pin	1	16	S-Cam Shaft	1
4	Slack Adjuster	1	17	Shoe Return Spring	1
5	Yoke	1	18	Anchor Spring	2
6	Cotter Pin	1	19	Spider	1
7	Washer	1	20	Dust Shield	2
8	Grease Seal	2	21	Rubber Inspection Plug	2
9	Bushing	2	22	Cap Nut	6
10	Cap Screw	4	23	Star Washer	6
11	Lock Washer	4	24	Actuator	1
12	Chamber Bracket And Cam Tube	1	25	Mounting Nuts	2
13	Brake Shoe Assembly	2	26	Washers	2

S-cam brake system components. *(Courtesy: Bendix Corp.)*

the drums. Cam type brake operation is accomplished by the transferal of torque through the slack adjuster camshaft assembly.

An S-cam is mounted on the brake shoe side of the camshaft. When the S-cam is rotated, it lifts the cam rollers and spreads the brake shoes apart in equal proportion, actuating contact with the brake drum. The brake assembly is held together by a series of hold-down springs, pins, and return springs, anchored by the brake spider assembly.

Disassembly

Park the truck on a level working surface and prevent truck movement by means other than the brakes.

WARNING: If the service brake chamber is equipped with a spring brake, follow the manufacturer's recommendations for caging the unit before servicing. Failure to do so can lead to serious injury.

Completely depressurize the air brake system. Raise and safely support the axle to be serviced. Back off the slack adjuster completely and remove the wheel and drum. Pry one of the shoes away from the cam roller and remove the pin and roller. Repeat this process on the opposite shoe. Inspect the cam roller. If it shows any wear, pitting or damage, replace it. Remove and discard the return springs.

Remove the shoes from the anchor pins. Slide the anchor pins out of the brake spider assembly.

CAUTION: When removing the anchor pins, don't heat the spider and try to hammer them out. Heating removes the metal's temper and hammering a hot spider will cause permanent distortion, reduced brake performance and abnormal wear. If the anchor pins are stubborn, douse them with a light, penetrating oil, let the oil work in and tap them out as gently as possible. Or, use a puller designed for that purpose.

Remove the slack adjuster assembly from the splined end of the brake camshaft. Then, remove the camshaft from its tube. If there is damage, mark and remove the dust shields from the spider assembly. Remove the actuator bracket and cam tube from the spider assembly, and replace the camshaft grease seals and bushings.

Cleaning And Inspection
ACTUATOR BRACKET AND CAM TUBE

Inspect the actuator bracket making sure it is not bent, and inspect the cam tube for broken or cracked welds. Inspect the camshaft bushings. If you determine that one bushing is worn, replace both bushings. Check all bearings and surfaces for signs of wear or damage.

CAMSHAFT

Check the camshaft splines for cracks and deformity. Replace the shaft if necessary. Check the bearing journals for wear or signs of damage. Replace the shaft if it is visibly worn or rough to the touch. Look carefully at the S-cam for flat spots and irregularities. An irregular surface on these parts will cause brake noise and make brakes 'grabby' and slow to release.

BRAKE SPIDER

Clean the brake spider with a solvent and/or wire brush, and inspect for broken welds or cracks in the camshaft and anchor pin areas. Check the tightness of the spider securing bolts, and be sure the spider is not bent. The anchor pin holes must be parallel to the centerline of the axle; otherwise, the shoes won't track properly in the drum, and the result will be tapered wear.

ROLLERS AND PINS

Look carefully at the rollers for flat spots and irregularities. An irregular surface on these parts will cause brake noise and make brakes 'grabby' and slow to release.

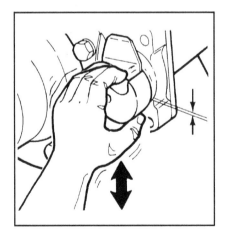

Wiggle the S-cam up-and-down to check for radial play. Most manufacturers recommend no more than a few hundredths of an inch play. More can cause uneven application and brake chatter.
(Courtesy: ArvinMeritor Corp.)

SHOES AND LINING

Make sure the brake shoes are not bent or cracked. Check the lining mounting holes and make sure they are not elongated.

Lining wear should be even around the circumference of the brake assembly, and inboard-to-outboard. More wear on the bottom, on top or on one side could very likely indicate that peripheral brake hardware is worn. If that is the case, the brakes cannot be properly adjusted. Look for tapered wear, a condition in which the shoes show more wear at the inboard or outboard side. Don't confuse tapered lining wear with a high ridge on the inside edge of the linings. This is actually beneficial, as it prevents a lip being etched into the drum and makes drum removal easier. It also helps keep water and contaminants out of the brake assembly.

Unequal lining wear between the leading and trailing ends of a shoe may be the result of a weak return spring, a worn outer S-cam bushing, or an out-of-arc shoe. Attempting to adjust a brake with any of these conditions will result in dragging and high contact pressure at one spot of the lining. This will lead to rapid lining wear and heat damage to the drum.

Replace the linings if unusually patterned cracks are found and the lining measures less than 1/4-in. at its lowest point. Make sure the lining is secured to the shoe and that the rivet holes are not unusually worn. Check the lining for foreign material that may be imbedded.

If linings are contaminated with oil or grease, correct the cause before relining. The problem is almost always a leaking oil seal, too much grease on a grease-type wheel bearing or camshaft bushing or the result of careless handling. If the lining is otherwise okay, but an area no larger than 10% of the total lining area is contaminated by grease or oil, the spot can be cleaned with brake cleaning solvent (not gasoline or another substitute). However, this is not the safest option, as it could lead to a brake imbalance condition if done improperly.

BRAKE DRUMS

A brake drum with surface heat checks should be periodically inspected. The checks may wear away, but if it's obvious that they're getting worse, discard the drum. Light scoring and abrasion are acceptable, as long as marks are no deeper than 0.010-in. Any crack that goes through the drum's thickness means that the drum should be discarded immediately and replaced.

To check for roundness, use a dial indicator to measure a mounted drum's inside diameter (ID) in the center of the rubbing path. Take another measurement 90 degrees from the first one, again in the center of the rubbing path. If the two measurements are not within 0.010-in. of each other, the drum can be resurfaced or rotated one bolt hole and rechecked. If it is severely out-of-round, the drum should be discarded.

It is permissible to resurface a heavy-duty drum to 0.080-in. over its minimum thickness, but bear in mind that the radius of the new lining may not match that of the drum. Reduced braking performance and lining damage can result.

Also remember that one of a drum's jobs is to absorb heat, and the heavier the drum, the more heat it can absorb. Resurfacing a drum removes valuable metal and reduces the drum's effectiveness. It is recommended to replace drums as wear approaches 0.080-in.

Clean wheel bearings with clean solvent, and inspect the races for signs of galling or brinelling. If the bearings do not rotate smoothly, replace them. Be sure the proper lubricant is used when they're reinstalled.

Assembly

Mount the spider and be sure it is properly oriented (front and back sides). Replace the camshaft bushings. Replace the seals in the camshaft end tube and chamber bracket, making sure the lip of the seal is facing inwards on both sides. Install the cam tube into the spider assembly. Reinstall the dust shields if removed.

Coat the camshaft journals with suitable lubricant and install the camshaft into the tube, taking care not to damage the seals. Install the slack adjuster assembly onto the splined end of the shaft. Install anchor pins into the spider assembly. When reassembling, don't forget to lube the cam bearing and seals, and anchor pin bores and bushings.

Install new brake shoe return springs. Install the brake shoes onto the spider assembly so that the top ends engage the anchor pins and the bottom ends engage the S-cam assembly. Install the brake shoe return spring onto the return spring pins of the opposite shoe. Pry the shoes out until the roller and pin can be installed between the S-cam and the slots in the end of the shoes. Reinstall the brake drum and wheel.

Disc Brakes

Air disc brake technology improves in-lane braking stability as compared to S-cam brakes. Small variations in lining friction or the drum surface on S-cam brakes can affect braking stability. Air disc brakes are designed to minimize this instability as pressure is applied constantly and efficiently to all wheels.

When the brakes are applied, the air chamber pushrod engages the automatic slack adjuster. The slack adjuster rotates the camshaft, which causes the camshaft nut to slide out along the camshaft. The nut pushes the piston and the inboard lining against the disc rotor. The force of the inboard lining pulls the caliper along its slide pins or mounting. The caliper movement forces the outboard pad to make contact with the disc rotor.

Caliper Removal

WARNING: If the service brake chamber is equipped with a spring brake, follow the manufacturer's recommendations for caging the unit before servicing. Failure to do so can lead to serious injury.

Completely depressurize the air brake system. Relieve the adjustment on the slack adjusters. Remove the caliper top slide pin (if equipped) and install it through the outboard caliper boss and into the torque plate to support the caliper. Remove both clevis pins from the slack adjuster. Remove the air chamber from its bracket. Remove the cotter pin from the bottom slide pin retainer and loosen the nut on the retainer.

Apply a suitable lubricant to help loosen the retainer. Press the end of the retainer to release the slide pin. Pull the bottom slide pin (if equipped) out of the caliper and torque plate. Pull the bottom of the caliper from the rotor and support the caliper. Remove the top slide pin and lift the caliper away from the rotor.

Caliper Installation

Support the caliper while aligning the bores in the top of the caliper to the torque plate. From the outboard side, install the slide pin (if equipped) into the top of the caliper and into the torque plate.

NOTE: The notch in the slide pin must be aligned with the retainer.

Push down the retainer and push in the slide pin (if equipped). The pin must extend past the inboard boss of the caliper. Tighten the slide pin retainer nut. Repeat this process to install the lower pin.

Some disc brake calipers are mounted directly to the torque plate by means of a retainer. This type of setup doesn't require slide pins. The top of the caliper is mounted underneath a lip on the torque plate, and the bottom of the caliper is held to the torque plate by installing the retainer. Instead of sliding on the pins, the caliper slides along the grooves in the torque plate.

Disc Brake Rotor

NOTE: Most manufacturers do not recommend resurfacing heavy-duty rotors. However, the practice can be safely performed in order to remove small imperfections in the rotor surface.

Inspect the disc rotor for heat cracks, grooves or scores, and blue marks (excessive heat). Light scoring and abrasion are acceptable, as long as they are no deeper than 0.010-in.

Using a micrometer, measure the thickness of the rotor. Measure thickness of the rotor in several places around its circumference. Discard the rotor if the measurement is less than 0.040 over the minimum manufacturer's specified thickness, or if the measurements vary more than 0.005-in.

Using a dial indicator, measure for lateral runout. If runout exceeds manufacturer's specifications, resur-

face or replace the rotor.

To remove the rotor, place a container under the end of the axle to capture leaking lubricant. Remove the hub cover and gasket. Remove the disc and wheel hub from the spindle, and separate the disc from the hub assembly.

Wheel Bearings

It is important to remember that in addition to malfunctioning brake system parts, worn hubs and wheel bearings can also contribute to poor braking performance. Many apparent braking problems that persist

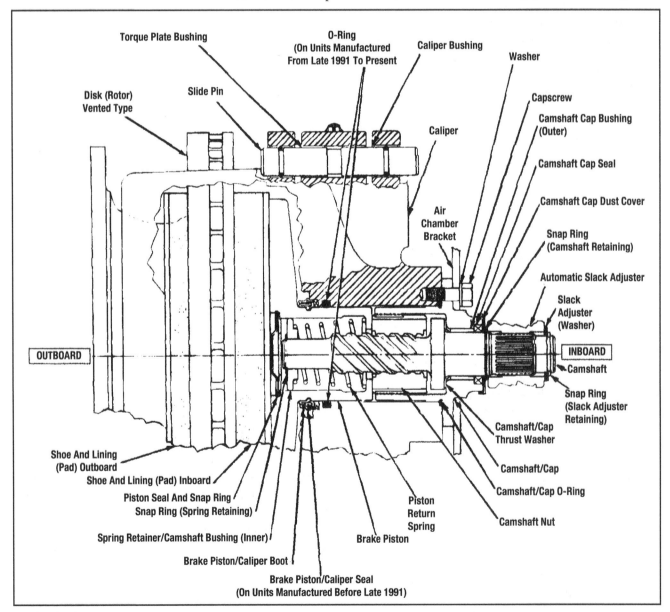

Air disc brake cutaway view. *(Courtesy: ArvinMeritor Corp.)*

after all the worn brake parts have been replaced can actually be caused by misadjusted or worn out wheel bearings.

There are two basic types of wheel ends, unitized and conventional. Unitized wheel ends are a complete packaged system with bearings, seals, and lubricant. Since the bearing adjustment is pre-set at the manufacturer, if there is a malfunction, the entire wheel end must be replaced.

Inspection procedures are basically the same for both unitized and conventional wheel ends. When the wheel bearings are inspected for looseness on any axle, be sure the brakes are fully released and the axle is safely raised off the floor. To inspect the bearings for excessive play, grasp the tire at the top and move it back and forth, or place a bar under the tire assembly and lift the bar and release it. If looseness in the bearings is present, the wheel assembly will move laterally.

Note the movement of the drum or rotor in relation to a stationary part of the brake backing plate or a suspension component. Compare the wheel movement against manufacturer's specifications.

Conventional, adjustable wheel end systems use standard bearings with an adjusting nut to set the bearing. Two types of bearings are used, ball bearings or tapered roller bearings. Generally, tapered rollers are somewhat more forgiving and tolerant of pre-set torque. Pre-adjusted systems are available with the bearings and seals pressed into the hubs. Adjustments can also be made when the adjusting nut and hardware are installed.

If the vehicle is equipped with a conventional wheel end, adjust the bearing by first preloading the bearing to the cup and then releasing the

Different types of bearing wear.

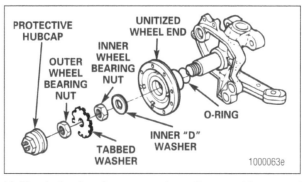

Unitized wheel end components.   *(Courtesy: Meritor, Inc.)*

preload. Tighten the adjusting nut to obtain the average allowed play, or the play specified by the manufacturer.

Different types of adjusting nuts and locking nut assemblies are used for the front and rear bearings. Do not attempt to interchange or mismatch the locking nut assemblies since locking capability can be lost. If a castellated nut assembly is used, torque in accordance with manufacturer's recommendations and install a new cotter pin. Never reuse the old one.

Both grease and oil-type lubrication is used with wheel bearings. Be sure of the type that is used on the vehicle before attempting to lubricate.

Replace wheel oil seals at the first sign of leakage, when lubricant needs to be added frequently or whenever

disassembly is necessary.

If you suspect a bad bearing in a conventional wheel end, remove the bearing and carefully inspect the working surfaces of not only the bearing, but also the spindle and hub assembly. You are looking for two flaws, abrasion damage and discoloration, such as heat bluing.

Abrasion damage can be the beginning of a crack that would allow the spindle or hub to fail catastrophically. Metal bluing discoloration indicates a change in the internal crystalline structure of the metal. It has become hardened and is no longer strong enough to support the kinds of forces transmitted through a wheel/hub/spindle assembly.

PARKING BRAKES

In addition to applying the service brakes used in everyday driving, the brake chambers on the rear tractor axles and on the trailer axles apply the parking brakes. These brake chambers (spring brakes), incorporate a second chamber containing a second diaphragm and a powerful spring.

WARNING: If the service brake chamber is equipped with a spring brake, follow the manufacturer's recommendations for caging the unit before servicing. Failure to do so can lead to serious injury.

Typical caging procedures require that the spring inside the chamber be mechanically captured to avoid accidental releasing. It is also important not to drop the spring brake because the high-tension spring may cause the chamber to fly apart, causing personal injury and/or physical damage to surroundings. If the spring brake is damaged in any way, do not attempt to cage it.

A commercially available release tool can be inserted through a hole in the brake chamber. Lock the tool into place. Install the release tool washer and nut and snug the nut to manufacturer's specifications. At this time, the caging procedure is complete. Remove the chamber using the manufacturer's procedures and release the spring using an approved safety chamber before discarding.

When the vehicle is in use, the dash-mounted parking brake valves are in the RUN (pushed-in) position. This supplies air pressure to the spring chamber on the side of the diaphragm opposite the spring. Air pressure acting on the diaphragm compresses the spring and the parking brakes are held off. This does not affect the operation of the service brakes.

When the vehicle is parked, the dash valves are pulled out. This exhausts spring brake hold-off air, allowing the spring to apply the parking brakes. In the event of a loss of system pressure, hold-off air pressure is, in most cases, overcome by the parking brake spring, and the brakes are automatically applied to provide emergency stopping.

Per Federal Motor Vehicle Safety Standards (FMVSS), the parking brakes must be able to hold a truck, loaded to its gross weight rating, stationary on a smooth, dry, concrete roadway, facing uphill or downhill on a 20-percent grade. In the emergency mode, the parking brakes must be able to exert a retarding force equal to 28 percent of gross axle rating.

Push-Pull Valves

A defective push-pull valve can cause premature spring brake application, slow brake release and brake drag.

The dash mounted push-pull valve, which controls parking brakes on the truck or tractor, and air supply to the trailer, comes in two styles, singular or dual integrated. On a straight truck, a single unit with a yellow parking brake

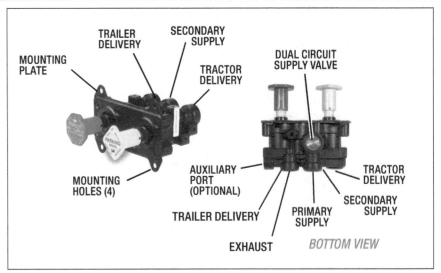

Typical dash mounted push-pull valve.
(Courtesy: Bendix Commercial Vehicle Systems)

knob is used to control the application of the parking brakes. When the valve is pushed in, air is supplied to the truck spring brake chambers to release the parking brakes. When the valve is pulled out, air pressure will exhaust from the spring brakes, actuating the parking brakes.

The dual unit controls the parking brakes on the tractor and the air supply on the trailer. When both valves are in, air is supplied to the tractor and trailer spring brake chambers to release the parking brakes. The parking brakes can be applied on both the tractor and trailer by pulling the yellow valve out. When the valve is pulled, air pressure will exhaust from the spring brakes, actuating the parking brakes. When the driver or technician wishes to uncouple the trailer, the red trailer air supply button should be pulled out.

Supply pressure to the trailer is prevented from being delivered, causing the tractor protection valve to function and closing off the signal line. In this position, the tractor can be operated without the trailer (bobtail). If the tractor is still coupled with the trailer, this action will apply the trailer parking brakes.

Diagnosis

FUNCTIONALITY CHECKS

Along with the leakage checks, the push-pull valve should be inspected for proper function. To do so, perform the following checks:

- When the red trailer supply knob is pulled out, the yellow parking brake knob should remain in
- With both knobs pushed in, pull out the yellow parking brake knob. The red trailer knob should pop out
- Completely depressurize the system. Install pressure gauges and monitor delivery pressure. Build up the pressure to 120 psi. Push the yellow parking brake knob in. Gauge delivery pressure should equal that of primary reservoir pressure
- Slowly depressurize the primary system and monitor the delivery pressure. It should drop at the same rate as the primary system pressure
- Recharge the system until secondary pressure is at around 120 psi, and primary pressure is around 100 psi. Slowly depressurize the secondary circuit. Spring brake pressure should equalize itself to that of the primary system pressure

• Build up the system pressure to 120 psi, pull out the red trailer supply knob and push in the yellow parking brake knob. Slowly depressurize the spring brake delivery line while holding the yellow parking brake control knob in. During depressurization, the air supply valve should operate.

LEAKAGE CHECKS

Gain access to the valve by removing the knobs (if necessary) and instrument panel covers. Charge the air system to no lower than 65 psi. Using soapy water, inspect for leakage at the body and cover plate. There should be no leakage.

Reinstall the knobs and push the yellow knob in. Coat the exhaust port with soapy water and observe the leakage. Leakage should not exceed a 1-in. soap bubble in five seconds. (See alternative test method information on page 14.)

Next, create a leak at the trailer service line by loosening one of the fittings. Inspect the trailer supply knob. It should pop out when the supply pressure drops to 20-45 psi. After the knob pops out, the supply pressure should stabilize. Close off the trailer supply line leak.

Reopen the trailer supply line leak and hold the red button in. Air should exhaust from the trailer valve exhaust port when the pressure drops to 25-35 psi.

Close off the trailer supply line leak and rebuild the pressure to at least 45 psi. Push the yellow knob in. The knob should remain in. Check for leakage at the parking valve exhaust port. It should not be more than 1-in. soap bubble in five seconds.

Build air pressure to at least 45 psi and create a leak in the tractor supply circuit. The yellow parking brake knob should pop out when the pressure drops to 20-30 psi. When the knob pops out, pressure should stabilize.

The push-pull valve can be replaced by completely depressurizing the air brake system and removing the control knobs and instrument panel covers. Mark and disconnect all air lines. Remove the control valve from its bracket and carefully remove the valve from its housing. After replacing the valve, start the engine and build up pressure until the governor cuts-out. Check for leaks and proper operation.

Notes

Hydraulic Brakes Diagnosis and Repair

When a hydraulic system is used, the only mechanical leverage that is used is in the foot pedal linkage and the parking brake linkage (in most cases). But an additional increase in ratio is achieved by varying the diameter of the wheel cylinders or caliper diameters in relation to the master cylinder bore diameter.

For example, if one wheel cylinder piston has an area of 2-in. square and another piston has an area of 1-in. square, and the system pressure is 400 psi, the 2-in. square piston will push against the brake shoes with a force of 800 pounds. The 1-in. square piston, however, will exert a force of only 400 pounds.

The ratio between the areas of the master cylinder and the wheel cylinders or calipers determines the multiplication of force at the pistons. If the master cylinder bore diameter is increased and the applying force remains the same, less pressure will be developed in the system. However, a larger wheel cylinder piston could be used to achieve the desired pressure at the wheel cylinder.

Obviously, a replacement master cylinder, wheel cylinder or caliper must be of the same design and bore diameter as the original unit.

There are several varieties of hydraulic brakes used on light- and medium-duty commercial trucks. Virtually all heavy-duty trucks use air-actuated brake systems.

Hydraulic systems are not well suited to heavy-duty applications for two reasons:

- A large volume of fluid would be needed to actuate, for instance, ten wheel cylinders (on an 18-wheeler)
- Coupling/uncoupling trailers would be messy, and fluid

leakage at the tractor/trailer connection while the vehicle is moving, could be disastrous. All hydraulic brake systems contain a fluid reservoir, a master cylinder, hydraulic lines and hoses, and one or more wheel cylinder(s) or brake calipers at each wheel.

Advantages of hydraulic brake systems in light- and medium-duty applications include:

- Immediate actuation with very little or no time delay due to the fact that fluid cannot be compressed
- High line pressures, which permit the use of smaller braking components
- Less initial expense due to smaller and fewer components.

HYDRAULIC SYSTEMS

Hydraulic system component malfunctions can lead to overall poor brake system performance.

If the vehicle is experiencing poor stopping or erratic brake application and release, suspect a defective brake master cylinder, misadjusted pedal pushrod, hydraulic fluid leaks, misrouted or restricted brake lines and hoses, air in the system, contaminated brake fluid or sticking wheel cylinder and/or caliper pistons.

If the front of the vehicle dives when the brakes are applied or if the front brake pads are extremely worn, suspect a defective metering or combination valve. A defective valve will cause the front brakes to activate too quickly. When operating properly, the valve delays front brake operation until the rear brakes begin to operate.

If, on moderate to hard brake application, the rear brakes lock

up or if the rear suspension has been modified, suspect a defective or out-of-adjustment load proportioning or combination valve. The valve provides maximum braking balance based on the truck's payload. As the load increases, brake pressure to the rear wheels is increased.

Master Cylinder

A defective or leaking brake master cylinder can lead to poor stopping ability or erratic brake application and release.

The master cylinder is the first link in the hydraulic chain. Its purpose is to transform the driver's foot application force at the brake pedal into hydraulic pressure. One master cylinder piston and reservoir component actuates the brakes on one axle, with a separate piston and reservoir compartment used to actuate the brakes on the other axle(s).

Since the front brakes do the most braking work, a failure in the front system would leave little reserve braking power. This problem was resolved with the advent of the diagonally split brake system. The diagonal system provides braking power to one front wheel and an opposite rear wheel.

This system is designed to leave at least 50% of the braking power at the driver's disposal. Of course, the truck should not be driven any further than necessary before the brake system is repaired.

Diagnosis

To check for an internal leak past the piston cups in the master cylinder, exhaust the brake booster vacuum by applying the brakes several

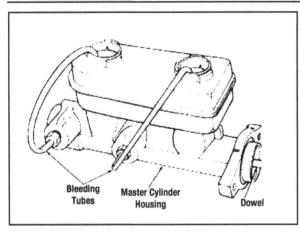

Bleeding the master cylinder. *(Courtesy: Bendix Corp.)*

times with the engine off. Hold steady pressure on the pedal. If the pedal sinks gradually, check wheel cylinders, hoses and connections for external leaks. If no leakage is visible, internal seals in the master cylinder have failed.

Removal

Disconnect and plug the primary and secondary lines of the master cylinder. Remove the master cylinder mounting nuts at the vacuum booster. Slide the master cylinder away from the vacuum booster assembly. Plug the brake lines that attach to the master cylinder in order to prevent system contamination. Remove the reservoir assembly and gasket (if equipped).

Bench Bleeding

Before a replacement master cylinder is installed, it must be independently bled (bench bled). Install the reservoir assembly with a new gasket (if equipped). Carefully clamp the master cylinder in a vise using soft-jaw clamps.

Attach special bleeding tubes to the primary and secondary ports of the master cylinder and fill both reservoirs with the specified brake fluid. Using a wood dowel, slowly depress the pushrod or piston while keeping the open bleeding tube ends submerged in the brake fluid. Allow the master cylinder piston to return under spring pres-

sure. You may need to perform this operation several times.

While bench bleeding, watch the fluid for air bubbles. Repeat the operation until no bubbles can be seen being expelled from the bleeding tubes. Remove the bleeding tubes and plug the ports. It's a good practice to reinstall the master cylinder cap at this time to prevent spillage or contamination of the brake fluid.

Installation

Install the master cylinder over the studs on the vacuum power brake unit and install the nuts. Install the primary and secondary brake lines and tighten to manufacturer's specifications. Bleed the entire brake system.

Brake Pedal Pushrod Adjustment

The pushrod is attached to the brake pedal and extends through the bulkhead to the brake booster. A pushrod that extends too far partially actuates the master cylinder and seals off the master cylinder compensating port. This will prevent pressurized fluid in the system from re-entering the master cylinder, leading to brake drag and pre-

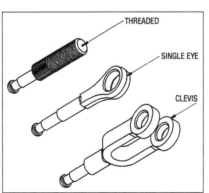

Typical brake pedal pushrods. *(Courtesy: Robert Bosch, Inc.)*

mature brake wear.

Push rod adjustment is accomplished either by means of an adjustment screw or nut (if applicable) or by installing shims between the master cylinder and power booster. There are two methods to confirm the correct adjustment, gauge and air.

Position a GO-NO-GO gauge over the piston rod. If the rod height is not within gauge limits, adjust the rod to specifications.

To air test the rod adjustment, apply approximately 5 psi to the hydraulic outlet of the master cylinder and watch the fluid. If air bubbles are seen coming from the smaller of the two holes (compensating port) of the master cylinder reservoir, adjustment is satisfactory. If air does not flow through the port, adjustment is required.

Brake Lines And Hoses

A leaking brake line or hose will cause depletion of brake fluid leading to poor stopping ability and pulling if the leak occurs at one of the wheel positions. In addition, a misrouted or malfunctioning hose or line can cause premature wear, grabbing or dragging.

Most brake line tubing is made up of double-wall steel, ranging in diameter from 1/8-in. to 3/8-in. There are a variety of fittings used to connect the tubing to junction blocks, valves and other tubing sections.

Proper tube flaring is vital in maintaining the integrity of the brake line. If any part of a brake line is damaged, the entire section should be replaced with tubing of the same type, size, shape and length.

The inverted flare style is the most common. Single flare or sleeve compression fittings may not provide adequate service in the demanding operating environment of a vehicle braking system. Always replace original equipment fittings with the exact same replacement.

Inspection

Brake manufacturers recommend that a visual inspection for hose and line wear, chafed or badly routed lines and hoses and other obvious damage is made whenever any brake service is required. However, it is also recommended that the driver perform a daily visible inspection.

Of course, a leak is the main reason to replace a line or a hose. However, there are other tell-tale signs that a hose should be replaced. A flexible brake hose should be replaced if it shows signs of softening, cracking or other damage. Cracking and physical damage may be obvious signs, but softening of the brake hose could be a symptom of an internally collapsed hose. While the outside of the hose may look acceptable, the inside may be collapsed to the point that it will not allow the proper amount of brake fluid to the brake components. Improper routing, clamping and crimping are cause for replacement. When installing a new brake hose, position the hose to avoid contact with other vehicle components.

Replacement

It is not recommended, and in most cases, illegal to splice or patch a leaking brake line or hose. Hoses must be replaced with DOT approved material intended for the specific application. Also, do not change the diameter of a hose or line. It is important to properly route a hose or line to avoid bending, kinking and wear-through problems. When bending brake tubing to fit the frame or rear-axle contours, be careful not to kink or crack the tube. After the line or hose is replaced, bleed the entire brake system.

Metering Valve

A defective or leaking metering valve will cause the front brakes to activate too quickly, causing front brake grab and premature front brake wear.

A brake metering valve is used on front disc/rear drum brake systems for the purpose of providing simultaneous application of all brakes. The valve is located in the front brake hydraulic circuit, and delays front brake operation until the rear brakes begin to operate. When the rear brakes make contact with the drum, hydraulic pressure in the front circuit will open the metering valve sending pressurized fluid to the front brakes.

Diagnosis

Road test the truck and apply the brakes. Note that upon application, the front of the truck does not dive. Stop the truck, and with the engine running, slowly apply the brakes. At approximately 1-in. of travel, a very small change in pedal effort should be detected if the valve is operating properly. This is due to the additional hydraulic pressure necessary to open the valve and allow fluid to reach the front calipers. To replace the valve, disconnect the brake lines and remove it from its mounting. Install a new valve, reconnect the lines and bleed the entire brake system.

Proportioning Valve

A defective or leaking load proportioning valve will cause rear brake lockup during moderate to hard brake application, brake drag, grabbing and premature rear brake wear.

The load proportioning valve provides maximum braking balance based on the truck's payload. It is located on the frame, and responds to changes in the chassis height based on rear axle load. As the load increases, brake pressure to the rear wheels is increased. The valve is linked to a bracket on the axle by mechanical linkage. Be careful that any modification made to the truck's suspension will not trick the proportioning valve into adjusting hydraulic pressure incorrectly.

Diagnosis

Road test the truck without a load. Upon light brake application, the rear brakes should stop proportionately with the front brakes. If the rear brakes lock too prematurely, the load proportioning valve is suspect.

Check the linkage adjustment by parking the unloaded truck on a level surface. Loosen the adjustment bracket and remove the slack

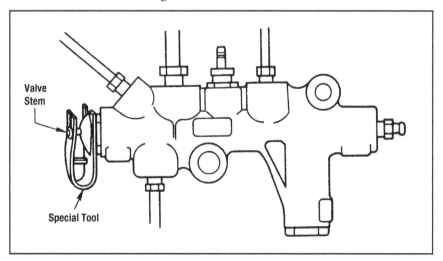

When pressure bleeding a disc/drum system, the metering valve must be open. Shown here is a special tool used to hold the valve open.

from the spring linkage that connects the axle to the valve.

If it is possible, bounce the truck up and down several times and observe the proportioning valve lever. If it does not move, it may be sticking due to rust or corrosion. If the lever is binding, try to loosen it. If the lever will not loosen, replace the valve.

Connect a high-pressure hydraulic gauge to the inlet line of the master cylinder and another gauge on the outlet line to the rear brakes. Disconnect the linkage from the valve, apply the brake pedal and check the readings against manufacturer's specifications.

To replace the valve, disconnect the lines and linkage, and unbolt the valve from its mounting. After replacement, reconnect the hydraulic lines, bleed the entire brake system and check adjustment.

Combination Valve

The combination valve is a single unit incorporating the metering and proportioning valves in conjunction with the pressure differential switch. Two-function valves incorporate either the proportioning valve and the pressure differential warning light function, or the metering valve and the brake pressure differential warning light function.

Three-function valves incorporate the proportioning valve, metering valve, and the brake pressure differential warning light function.

Diagnosis is similar to the metering valve and proportioning valve diagnosis. If either function operates improperly, the entire unit must be replaced. To replace the unit, disconnect the hydraulic lines and switch wire and remove the valve from its mounting. After replacement, re-connect the hydraulic lines and wire, and bleed the entire brake system.

Pressure Differential Switch

The pressure differential warning switch alerts the driver of pressure loss in one of the hydraulic circuits by way of a warning light. Under

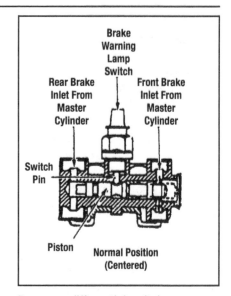

Pressure differential switch.

normal operating conditions, the hydraulic pressure on both sides of the pressure differential piston is balanced and the piston is centered. In this position, a spring-loaded plunger opens the contacts and keeps the brake warning light off. If one of the circuits develops a leak, the higher pressure in the other circuit will move the piston to one side. This causes the pres-

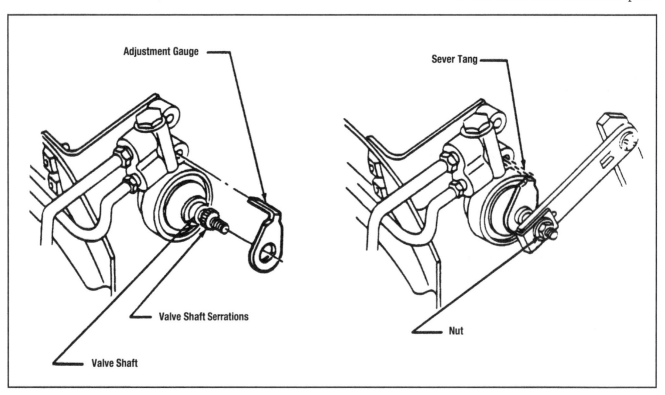

Adjusting the load proportioning valve.

sure differential switch to close, completing the circuit and illuminating the brake warning light. The switch may be mounted separately or incorporated in with the combination valve.

To replace the unit, disconnect the hydraulic lines and wire, and remove the switch or combination valve from its mounting. After replacement, re-connect the wire and hydraulic lines and bleed the entire brake system.

Wheel Cylinders

A leaking wheel cylinder can coat the brakes with hydraulic fluid causing poor stopping, pulling, grabbing, premature wear and brake drag. Wheel cylinders with seized pistons will not operate the brake shoes. This can cause brakes at other wheel positions to compensate, leading to premature wear.

Diagnosis

After removing the brake drum, inspect the wheel cylinder(s) for leakage around the dust boots. If possible, pull back the dust boots and inspect the inner side for leakage. Replace the wheel cylinder if hydraulic fluid leakage is found.

Another potential problem with a wheel cylinder is binding. This condition is generally the result of contaminated fluid. Deposits form inside the wheel cylinder bore and cause the pistons to jam. A telltale sign of piston binding is excessive wear on one of the shoes while the other shoe exhibits minimal wear.

If the pistons are binding in the applied position, most likely the drum will be hard to remove and the brakes will be excessively worn. If the pistons are binding in the released position, there will be almost no brake wear as opposed to the other wheel positions. Always inspect the wheel cylinder for binding, even if you don't find leakage.

Removal

On some models, the wheel cylinder can be replaced without removing the brake shoes. However, removal of the shoes is recommended. Raise and safely support the truck and remove the wheel and drum. Locate the brake line leading to the wheel cylinder and disconnect it. Remove the cylinder by releasing a hold-down clip or removing the mounting bolts on the back side of the backing plate. Withdraw the cylinder from the backing plate.

Installation

Mount the wheel cylinder onto the backing plate and secure with either the hold-down clip or the mounting bolts. Connect the brake line and reinstall the brake shoes so that they are properly positioned against the wheel cylinder pistons. Reinstall the drum and wheel and adjust the brakes. Bleed the entire brake system.

Disc Brake Caliper

A defective or leaking disc brake caliper can cause poor stopping ability, premature or uneven brake wear, pulling, grabbing or dragging.

Diagnosis

Inspect the caliper for signs of hydraulic fluid leakage at the dust boot. Check the connection to the caliper for leakage. Caliper seize is usually attributed to guide bolt or slider corrosion, or piston seizure. Check the guide bolts or sliders for lateral movement, making sure the sleeves move from side-to-side using moderate pressure.

Operate the brakes and note that the caliper piston(s) engage the brake pads smoothly and that the caliper slides freely on the guide pins (if equipped) or caliper mounting.

Removal

Drain about half the brake fluid from the master cylinder. Raise and safely support the truck and remove the wheels. Remove the brake line and check to see if there is a sealing washer (usually made of copper). Discard the sealing washer.

Remove the caliper mounting pins (if equipped) or retaining plate. Slide the caliper assembly out and away from the disc rotor.

Disassembly

NOTE: While it is possible to rebuild hydraulic disc brake calipers, most manufacturers recommend replacement.

Remove the brake pads from the caliper assembly. Insert a rag or shop towel between the outer edge of the piston(s) and the inner edge of the caliper body. Gradually apply compressed air to the inlet port of the caliper to remove the piston(s).

WARNING: To avoid injury, always make sure that the piston is facing down toward the bench when removing with compressed air, and keep hands away from the piston area.

In the event a piston is seized in the bore, tap the end of the piston with a soft-headed hammer or mallet before applying air pressure to the inlet.

Cleaning And Inspection

Inspect the caliper piston and bore for pitting, scoring and corrosion. If any of these conditions exist, replace the piston or caliper assembly. Remove the caliper bore O-ring and clean the bore with a suitable cleaner.

Assembly

Soak the piston O-ring in clean

brake fluid. Insert the O-ring into the caliper bore and gently work it until it is properly seated. Make sure the seal is not twisted in its seat. Coat the outer portion of the piston with clean brake fluid.

On some models, the dust boot can be installed onto the piston face lip, and the piston installed into the caliper bore using a C-clamp or appropriate tool. When the piston is seated in the bore, tap the outer boot ring with a soft-headed hammer until it is seated flush with the top of the piston bore. On other models, the dust boot can be installed in the caliper bore first by tapping the outer boot ring with a soft-headed hammer until it is seated flush with the top of the piston bore.

In either case, the piston can be pressed into place using a C-clamp or appropriate tool until it is bottomed into the bore and the dust boot is secured to the piston face lip.

Installation

Mount the brake pads into the caliper assembly being careful to notate brake pad orientation. Make sure the caliper mounting pins (if equipped) are clean before installing; this facilitates the back-and-forth sliding effort of the calipers when they operate.

Carefully lower the caliper over the disc brake rotor until it seats properly on its mounting. Install the brake line and new sealing washer (if equipped). Install the brake caliper retainer or brake pins (if equipped) and torque to manufacturer's specifications. Reinstall the wheel and tire and bleed the entire brake system.

NOTE: Some disc brake calipers are mounted directly to the torque plate by means of a retainer. This type of setup doesn't require slide pins. The top of the caliper is mounted underneath a lip on the torque plate, and the bottom of the caliper is held to the torque plate by installing the retainer. Instead of sliding on the pins, the caliper slides along the grooves in the torque plate.

Brake Fluid

The fact that fluids cannot be compressed does not mean that all brake fluids are the same. Because of the tremendous amount of heat generated by the brakes, a minimum boiling point is needed for brake fluid.

Brake fluid must meet specific standards set by the Department of Transportation (DOT) and the Society of Automotive Engineers (SAE) for boiling point, lubricity, corrosion protection, water tolerance and rubber compatibility.

The three grades of brake fluid are:
- DOT 3– 401°F minimum boiling point, glycol-based, hygroscopic
- DOT 4– 446°F minimum boiling point, glycol-based, hygroscopic
- DOT 5– 500°F minimum boiling point, silicone-based, non-hygroscopic.

The term hygroscopic is used to describe something that attracts moisture. Both DOT 3, and DOT 4 brake fluids share this characteristic. However, the primary advantage to silicone brake fluid is that it always retains its high boiling point due to its non-hygroscopic nature.

Additionally, the fact that DOT 5 does not absorb moisture means that hydraulic components will neither rust or pit in this type of fluid. The downside to silicone brake fluid is that it's prone to aeration. This means that when the fluid is agitated, tiny air bubbles like those found in a carbonated drink form in the fluid.

For this reason, DOT 5 brake fluid is never to be used in an antilock brake system. The tendency for aeration with DOT 5 makes brake bleeding a little more difficult. Silicone brake fluid is more prevalent in commercial trucks and can be recognized by its purple color.

To determine if contamination exists in the brake fluid, as indicated by swollen, deteriorated rubber cups, the following test can be performed: Place a small amount of the drained brake fluid into a small, clear glass bottle. Separation of the fluid into distinct layers will indicate mineral oil content.

Play it safe—discard old brake fluid that has been bled from the system. Fluid drained from the bleeding operation may contain dirt particles or other contaminants and should not be reused.

Bleeding The System

Never use brake fluid from a container that has been used for any other reason. Mineral oil, alcohol, antifreeze or cleaning solvents—even in very small quantities—will contaminate brake fluid. Contaminated brake fluid will cause deterioration of rubber components.

The primary and secondary hydraulic brake systems are bled separately. As a rule, bleed the longest line first on the individual system being serviced.

Remove the master cylinder reservoir cap. Attach a clear tube to the bleeder screw at the wheel cylinder or disc caliper. Immerse the hose in a small amount of clean brake fluid in a clean, clear container. Open the bleeding screw. If a pressure-bleeder is not available, have an assistant slowly pump the brakes at least three or four times and hold the pedal down firmly. Carefully open the bleeder screw, allowing brake fluid and air

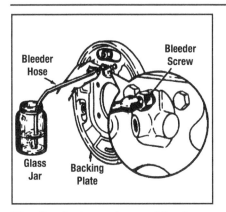

Bleeding brakes using a rubber hose and brake fluid in a clear container.

to escape. Once the brake pedal reaches the floor, close the bleeding screw. Repeat this operation until the fluid coming out of the rubber tube contains no air bubbles.

NOTE: When bleeding, always maintain a fluid level in the master cylinder. Never reuse brake fluid that has been drained from the hydraulic system.

Bleed the master cylinder at the outlet port of the system being serviced. On a master cylinder without bleed screws, loosen the hydraulic line securing nut. Operate the brake pedal slowly until the brake fluid at the outlet connection is free of bubbles, and then tighten the tube nut to the specified torque.

Do not use the secondary piston stop screw located on the bottom of some master cylinders to bleed the brake system. Loosening or removing this screw could result in damage to the secondary piston or stop screw. If the master cylinder has a bleeding screw, bleed in the same manner as a wheel cylinder.

Flushing The System

It is recommended that the entire hydraulic system be flushed with fresh brake fluid whenever new parts are installed, especially if brake fluid contamination is suspected.

Approximately one quart of fluid is required to do the job, but it's best to have more on hand. Additionally, the system must be flushed if there is any doubt as to the grade or integrity of the fluid in the system. Any rubber parts that have been exposed to contaminated brake fluid must be replaced. Remove the master cylinder reservoir cover and inspect the condition of the rubber diaphragm. Any swelling or distortion of the diaphragm is an indication that the brake fluid is contaminated.

As the brake fluid accumulates moisture over time, the brakes may operate normally when cold. However, under heavy prolonged braking, the fluid in the wheel cylinders and calipers will boil due to the water content. At the very least, this condition will create a spongy brake pedal. Besides moisture, the brake fluid can accumulate a host of other contaminants. Most of the time, this is the reason the brake fluid turns dark over time.

MECHANICAL SYSTEM

Hydraulic brake systems can experience mechanical component failure that will contribute to overall poor braking performance.

After a thorough road test, check to see if there are symptoms such as pulling to one side, grabbing too quickly, improperly releasing or poor stopping ability, the system could be experiencing what is called 'mechanical imbalance.'

When checking mechanical imbalance, the first thing to look for is improperly adjusted brakes. Brakes that are out of adjustment often display symptoms of more complex problems, especially when all the brakes are not adjusted to the same degree. This results in brake imbalance and increased stopping distance.

If the brakes are improperly ad-

justed, make sure the adjusters are working properly and adjust the brakes.

After the brakes are adjusted, if poor braking performance is still being experienced, look for inoperative brake chambers, inoperative or improperly adjusted slack adjusters (if equipped), worn brake hardware, cracked brake spiders, worn, tapered, glazed or cracked brake shoes, drums with scoring, cracking, excessive inside diameter (ID) and/or runout.

It is important to 'burnish' the brake shoes and/or pads after servicing. This process conditions the lining and establishes a uniform contact surface between the lining and drum and/or rotor. Follow the burnishing procedure recommended by the manufacturer.

In addition to being one of the friction elements, the brake drum (or rotor in disc brakes) also acts as a heat sink and a heat exchanger. It must rapidly absorb heat during braking, and hold it until it can be dissipated into the air. The heavier a drum or rotor is, the more heat it can hold. The hotter brake linings get, the more susceptible they are to brake fade, especially drum brakes. Brake fade is a condition of brake lining overheating and is potentially dangerous. When fade occurs, lining-to-drum friction is reduced and vehicle stopping distance is increased.

Different linings have different fade characteristics. Therefore, if mismatched linings are installed on different axles, brake action and balance are affected.

Brake Drum

As with air brake drums, hydraulic brake drums with surface heat checks should be periodically inspected. If the heat checks don't wear away in time, replace the drum. Light scoring should be no deeper than 0.010-in. Any crack

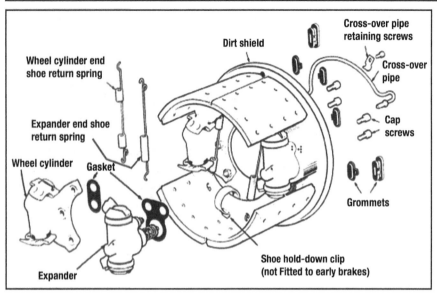

Hydraulic brake drum setup.   *(Courtesy: Bendix Commercial Vehicle Systems.)*

that goes through the drum's thickness means that the drum should be scrapped.

Use a dial indicator to measure a mounted drum's diameter in the center of the rubbing path. Take another measurement 90 degrees from the first one. If the two measurements are within 0.010-in. of each other, the drum can be resurfaced. Replace the drum if it is not within these resurfacing specifications.

It is permissible to resurface a drum to 0.060-in. oversize, but bear in mind that the radius of the new lining will not match that of the drum. Reduced braking performance and lining damage can result.

Also remember that the heavier the drum, the more heat it can absorb. Turning a drum removes valuable metal and reduces the drum's effectiveness. It is recommended to replace drums as wear approaches 0.060-in.

Clean wheel bearings with clean solvent, and inspect the races for signs of galling or brinelling. If they do not rotate smoothly, replace them. Be sure the proper lubricant is used when they're reinstalled.

Disc Brake Rotor

Resurface or replace a rotor if, after using a dial indicator, runout exceeds manufacturer's specifications. Inspect the disc rotor for heat cracks, grooves or scores and blue marks (excessive heat). Blue marks on the rotors indicate that the rotor at one time was excessively hot, probably due to a malfunction in the brake system. Light scoring and abrasion are acceptable, as long as they are no deeper than 0.010-in. Using a micrometer, measure the thickness of the rotor in several places around its circumference. Discard the rotor if the measurement is less than 0.040 over the minimum manufacturer's specified thickness, or if the measurements vary more than 0.005-in.

Brake Shoes

Worn out, cracked or inoperative brake shoes will lead to poor stopping, brake noise, pulling, grabbing and dragging.

Typical hydraulic drum brakes employ a pair of brake shoes mounted on a stationary backing plate. They are held in place by a series of springs and actuated by wheel cylinders. On most mod-

els, the adjuster is bolted to the backing plate. The return springs laterally secure the shoes allowing them to return to position after a brake application. The hold-down springs or retainers keep the shoes secured to the backing plates.

In the case of non-self-adjusting drum brakes; normal brake lining wear reduces pedal reserve. Low pedal reserve may also be caused by the lack of brake fluid in the master cylinder. The wear condition may be compensated by a minor brake adjustment, which moves the brake shoes closer to the insides of the drum. Master-cylinder fluid levels should be checked periodically.

Inspection

Raise and safely support the vehicle. Remove the wheel. Remove the adjuster hole plugs from the back of the backing plate. Using a tool specifically made for the application, turn the adjuster, backing the shoes off until they clear the drum. Remove the drum.

Make sure the brake shoes are not bent or cracked. Check the holes and make sure they are not elongated.

Lining wear should be even around the circumference of the brake assembly, and inboard-to-outboard. More wear on the bottom, on top, or on one side could very likely indicate that peripheral brake hardware is worn. If that is the case, brakes cannot be properly adjusted. Look for tapered wear, a condition in which the shoes show more wear at the inboard or outboard side. Unequal lining wear between the leading and trailing ends of a shoe may be the result of a weak return spring or an out-of-arc shoe. Attempting to adjust a brake with any of these conditions will result in dragging and high contact pressure at one spot of the lining. This will lead to rapid lin-

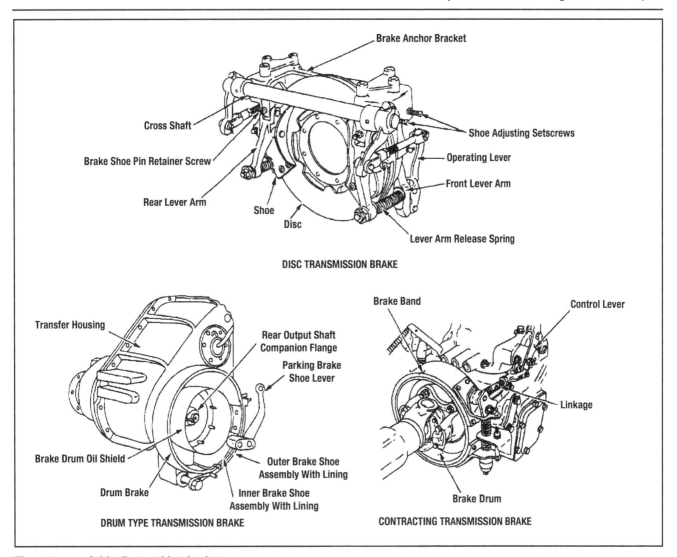

Three types of driveline parking brakes.

ing wear and heat damage to the drum.

Replace the linings if unusually patterned cracks are found and the lining measures less than 1/4-in. at its lowest point. Make sure the lining is secured to the shoe and that the rivet holes (if equipped) are not unusually worn. Check the lining for imbedded foreign material.

If linings are contaminated with brake fluid or grease, correct the cause. The problem is almost always a leaking oil seal, too much grease on a grease-type wheel bearing or a leaking wheel cylinder. If the lining is otherwise okay, but an area no larger than 10% of the total lining area is contaminated, the spot can be cleaned with brake cleaning solvent (not gasoline or another substitute). However, this isn't the safest option, as it could lead to a brake imbalance condition if done improperly.

Removal

Disconnect the brake shoe return springs. With the hold-down springs or retainers still attached, pull the brake shoes away from the wheel cylinder and adjuster assembly. If the adjuster assembly is independent of the backing plate, remove the adjuster. Remove the hold-down springs or retainers and remove the shoes. Inspect the wheel cylinder for leaks and the adjuster for proper operation. Check the parking brake expander (if equipped) for proper operation.

NOTE: Some drum brake adjusters are attached to the shoe in a similar fashion to that of an automobile, while others may be attached to the backing plate.

Installation

Install the brake shoes using the hold-down springs or retainers. If the adjuster is independent of the backing plate, install the adjuster and position the brake shoes over the wheel cylinder pistons. If the adjuster is part of the backing plate, position the brake shoes over the adjuster and the wheel cylinder pistons. Install the return springs using a tool specifically made for the application. Next, install the brake drum, along with the tire and wheel assembly. Adjust the brakes by inserting an adjustment tool into the backing plate and turning the adjustment wheel. Turn the adjuster assembly while spinning the tire and wheel until the brakes start to drag.

Low-pedal brake adjustment is required after installation of new or relined brake shoes. Adjustment is also necessary whenever excessive pedal travel is needed to start braking action. All hydraulic disc brakes are inherently self-adjusting, while most drum assemblies have a self-adjustment mechanism to keep brakes properly adjusted during normal vehicle operation.

Driveline Parking Brakes

The driveline parking brake is mounted at the rear of the transmission. While the operation of these brakes varies depending on the specific type of driveline parking brake setup, the basic principles are the same.

The braking mechanism, mounted on the rear of the transmission or transfer case, holds the truck by equalizing torque through the differential. When the brakes are applied, the brakes are expanded or contracted onto a drum or rotor holding the truck in place. The three styles most commonly used are disc, expanding shoe, and contracting shoe.

The driveline parking brake is actuated either by a hand-operated lever or a foot pedal.

To check the operation of the parking brake, park the truck on a flat surface and start the engine. Make sure the area in both the front and rear of the truck is clear. If the truck has an automatic transmission, place the gear selector in drive. The truck should not move. If the truck has a standard trans-

mission, place the shift lever in second gear and gradually engage the clutch assembly. The truck should not move.

Removal

With the truck in neutral and the wheels blocked, release the parking brakes and disconnect the linkage at the drum or rotor. Disconnect the driveline at the universal joint or yoke.

CONTRACTING SHOE

On contracting shoe type parking brakes, remove the adjusting bolts, cam levers and release spring at the shoe assembly. Remove the brake band and anchor clip spring.

EXPANDING SHOE

On expanding shoe type parking brakes, remove the U-joint flange at the brake drum and lift off the brake drum. Remove the parking brake shoe return springs and anchor pins. Expand the shoes enough to clear the support plate tabs and remove the shoes along with the adjuster and lower return spring.

DISC

After the parking brake linkage is disconnected, remove the parking brake shoe retracting spring and the rear shoe pivot pin along with the rear shoe assembly. Remove the front brake pivot pin and shoe assembly.

Installation

CONTRACTING SHOE

Install the anchor clip spring and slide the brake band over the brake drum. Install the adjusting bolts, cam levers and release spring. Reconnect the parking brake shoe linkage and install the driveline.

EXPANDING SHOE

Make sure the adjuster is working properly and install it onto the

shoes along with the bottom return spring. Be careful of the orientation of the spring so that it does not interfere with the adjuster operation. Expand the parking brake shoes enough to clear the support plate tabs and install behind the tabs. Install the upper return springs and anchor pins. Reconnect the parking brake linkage and install the driveline.

DISC

Install the front and rear brake shoes and pivot pins. Install the parking brake shoe retracting spring. Reconnect the parking brake shoe linkage and install the driveline.

Adjustment

CONTRACTING SHOE

Adjust the lower half of the brake band by turning the adjustment bolt that holds the band to the support until there is 1/32-in. clearance. Tighten the adjustment bolt locknut. Adjust the upper half of the brake band by turning the nuts at the bottom of the adjusting bolt. After the adjustment is made, lock the two nuts together.

EXPANDING SHOE

Block the wheels and release the parking brake. Raise and safely support one wheel. Fully release the parking brake shoes by removing the clevis pin. Rotate the drum until the adjustment access hole is in line with the adjuster. Using a suitable adjustment tool, rotate the adjuster to expand the shoes against the drum. Adjust the shoes until the fit is snug.

With the parking brake lever fully released, take up the slack in the linkage by pulling the lever just enough to overcome spring tension. Adjust the clevis, lining it up with the relay lever hole and insert the clevis pin along with a

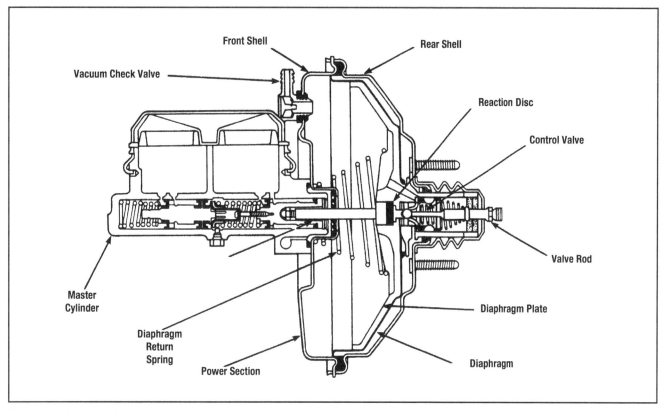

Cross section of a dual master cylinder and vacuum operated power brake booster.

new cotter pin. Tighten the clevis locknut.

DISC

Make sure the cable is disconnected from the lever. With the driveline removed, adjust the anchor screws until a slight drag is felt when inserting a 0.030-in. feeler gauge between the top end of the shoe and the rotor. Leaving the feeler gauge in place, tighten the adjusting nut until a slight drag is felt when inserting a 0.030-in. feeler gauge at the bottom end of the parking brake shoes. Remove the feeler gauges and spin the disc rotor. It should not drag. Install the driveline and the cable lever.

POWER ASSIST UNITS

In the event of a power-assist failure, the driver can experience increased effort to stop the vehicle. After a thorough road test, if you experience symptoms such as a hard brake pedal feel, dragging

brakes or brake fluid loss with no external leaks found, suspect an inoperative power-assist unit or brake booster.

Power brake boosters are designed to assist the driver during brake applications. It contains a diaphragm separating the two halves of the booster. Intake manifold or pump vacuum is supplied to the engine compartment side of the diaphragm, while brake pedal application operates an internal valve that regulates the amount of outside air introduced to the bulkhead side of the diaphragm.

When the brakes are not applied, the diaphragm is in a stationary position since vacuum exists. When the brake pedal is pushed, atmospheric pressure is introduced into the chamber on the bulkhead side of the diaphragm. This action causes a pressure differential, forcing the booster power piston forward, actuating the master cylinder. When the brake pedal is re-

leased, a spring in the booster returns the diaphragm to its original position.

The booster is connected to intake manifold vacuum on gasoline engines, and to a vacuum pump on diesel engines by way of a vacuum hose and one-way check valve. The valve is designed to maintain brake assist during periods of low vacuum.

Diagnosis

The first step in diagnosing and correcting brake trouble in a truck equipped with power brakes is determining whether the booster is at fault or whether the problem is in the brakes or hydraulic system. Here are some common problems and solutions:

HARD PEDAL

Connect a vacuum gauge to the engine manifold—not at the carburetor or throttle body. Or, if the truck has a diesel engine, connect the gauge to the suction port of the vacuum pump assembly. Allow the engine to run at idle speed. The gauge should show 18–20-in. of vacuum. If the vacuum reading is low, adjustments or repair to the engine may be required. On diesel engines, the vacuum pump may need servicing. Shut off the engine. If the gauge shows a drop of more than 2-in. in 3 minutes, the vacuum check-valve should be replaced.

Disconnect the vacuum hose from the power unit (booster). Connect the vacuum gauge to the hose on the booster-side of the check-valve, if possible, and check for leaks at the vacuum reservoir, hose or connections. If leaks are indicated by a drop in vacuum with the engine off, replace the hose, check-valve, connections or reservoir, if necessary.

With the engine shut off, apply the brake pedal several times to exhaust all vacuum from the system. Depress the brake pedal and hold while starting the engine; the pedal should tend to 'fall away' from your foot. If not, the vacuum portion of the power unit is not functioning. It should be replaced with a new or rebuilt unit that has been checked on a test bench.

DRAGGING BRAKES

Check the brake pedal to be sure it is fully released and is not binding. Check position of the brake light switch. It should not interfere with brake pedal travel.

Exhaust vacuum from the system by applying brakes several times with the engine shut off. Jack up both front wheels. Spin both wheels to be sure they are free. If not, check for stretched or missing return springs. Adjust brakes (if drums) and wheel bearings.

With the wheels spinning, start the engine but do not apply brakes. When the wheels stop spin-

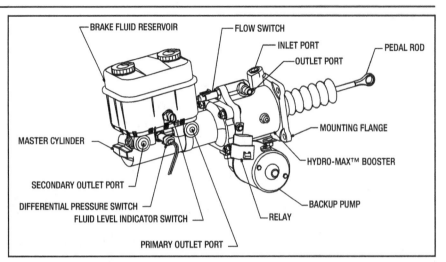

Hydro-Max booster assembly with backup electric pump.
(Courtesy: Robert Bosch, Inc.)

ning, check for drag. If drag is present, the power unit is defective.

FLUID LOSS/NO EXTERNAL SIGNS

Remove the hose between the intake manifold and power unit. Check for signs of hydraulic fluid. If the inside of the hose is wet from fluid, the power unit is defective. If the problem is not located after checking engine vacuum, power unit and connections, check the hydraulic system or foundation brake assembly.

If the hydraulic system is in good condition, check for excessive clearance between linings and drums.

Hydro-Assist Booster

The hydro-boost system is a variation on the conventional vacuum-assist system. It operates by using the power steering pump fluid pressure instead of manifold vacuum. The unit contains an open-center spool valve that regulates the amount of pressure, as the brakes are applied.

A lever controls the valve's position, while a boost piston provides the necessary force to operate the conventional master cylinder mounted to the front of the booster. An accumulator supplies a reserve of at least two assisted brake applications.

When normal hydraulic flow is interrupted, the internal reserve flow switch closes the backup pump electrical circuit. This energizes a relay, which activates the electric pump. The pump then provides reduced-rate fluid pressure for limited assist.

If the backup pump does not run, check for adequate voltage. If voltage is present, suspect a defective backup pump. Since the flow switch is the main activator of the backup pump, suspect the relay if the pump runs continuously.

When the driver applies the brakes, the pedal pushrod activates the spool valve, which directs power steering fluid to the piston and pushes it forward, helping to apply the brakes.

To check the system, pump the brakes several times with the engine off. Hold the pedal down firmly and start the engine. The pedal should fall slightly when the engine is started.

Some symptoms of booster failure include:
- Unacceptable brake pedal return
- Brakes grabbing
- Excessive brake pedal effort.

When replacing the booster, be sure the accumulator is depressurized according to manufacturer's procedures. Make sure the vehicle is parked on a level surface with the engine off and the negative battery cable disconnected.

Remove the master cylinder and set it aside. Disconnect the wiring from the backup pump and the flow switch. Disconnect the brake pedal pushrod. Next, remove the hydraulic supply and return lines. Finally, remove the booster retainers and booster from the bulkhead. After the booster is replaced and all components are properly reinstalled, bleed the system in strict accordance to manufacturer's service procedures.

Notes

Air And Hydraulic Antilock Brake Systems (Abs) and Automatic Traction Control (Atc), Electronic Stability Control Systems

Differences between antilock brake systems involve configuration, degree of complexity and cost. Individual wheel control is the most effective—and most expensive—form of ABS.

In this type of system, each wheel is independently monitored and controlled to take advantage of whatever level of adhesion is available to it. This is especially helpful in the event of a panic stop when there is a split coefficient of friction, such as a wet shoulder and dry crown.

The system will modulate the wheels on the wet side to avoid lock-up, and will go for maximum deceleration on the dry side. However, this will occur gradually to avoid throwing the truck sideways or wrenching the steering wheel from the driver's hands.

The number of channels in an individual-wheel-control system refers to the number of individual brakes its ECU (Electronic Control Unit) is capable of independently controlling. For example, a system that can independently accommodate all of the brakes on a steer axle and tandem is referred to as a 6-channel system. A 4-channel system can also be applied to a 3-axle truck, but the front and rear wheels on either side of the tandem would be braked simultaneously, rather than independently.

A select-low system typically is installed on drive axle(s), although the technology is adaptable to steer and trailer axle applications as well. In a select-low system, sensors at each axle end feed wheel-speed data to the ECU. When an impending skid condition is sensed at either the left or right wheel, the brakes at both wheels are modulated, rather than just those on the wheel that was

about to lock.

Advantages to this type of arrangement include simplicity and low cost. Since the drive axle(s) have a great impact on vehicle stability, a select-low system helps a driver retain control during emergency braking. One disadvantage is that, if the system is applied only to the drive axle, the front axle can still lock. Another disadvantage is that, in split situations, stopping distances may be longer than with an individual-wheel-control system. That's because the entire axle is braked as though both wheels were on the slippery surface.

All new-generation antilock systems 'fail soft'—that is, when they malfunction, the brake system simply behaves as though there was no ABS.

Although ABS works well when installed only on the tractor of a tractor/trailer combination, further safety benefits and improved tire life can be realized by adding ABS to trailers.

All antilock systems work in basically the same way. Inductive sensors, mounted at the wheel ends or in axle housings, pick up impulses from toothed rings that rotate with the wheels (or axles). These toothed rings are called tone wheels. The tone wheel is a metal wheel containing teeth that is mounted to each hub.

If the control module determines that wheel lock-up is about to take place, it will issue commands to a modulator. On hydraulic systems, wheel speed data is sent to an ECU, which sends an electrical signal to reduce hydraulic pressure to the affected wheel(s).

On air-operated systems, wheel speed data is sent to an ECU, which sends an electrical signal to reduce

air pressure to the brake chamber(s) at the affected wheels(s). The new rate of deceleration is recognized by the ECU, which signals the solenoid valves to restore air pressure. This loop occurs repeatedly, as long as the deceleration rate approaches lock-up.

The modulator is usually mounted to the frame fail or a crossmember.

Each sensor/wheel combination is kind of an electric generator, consisting of a permanent magnet and coil. As the rotating teeth pass a sensor, the magnetic signal picked up by the coil is intermittently altered. Alternating voltage is produced, the strength and frequency of which are proportionate to wheel speed.

On front axles, the wheel speed sensors are installed through the steering knuckle. On drive axles, they are mounted in a block attached to the axle housing.

AIR OPERATED ABS

Air operated antilock brakes operate similarly to hydraulic antilock brakes. The only difference is that compressed air is used as an actuator in place of hydraulic brake fluid. The National Highway Traffic Safety Administration (NHTSA) requires that ABS be installed on commercial trucks built (built meaning the official date of manufacture) on or after:
- March 1, 1997, for air-braked truck-tractors
- March 1, 1998, for other air-braked vehicles (trucks, buses, trailers and converter dollies).

Other aspects of NHTSA's rule stipulate that:
- New tractors—built on or after March 1, 1997—provide constant electrical power to a tractor-to-trailer electrical connector

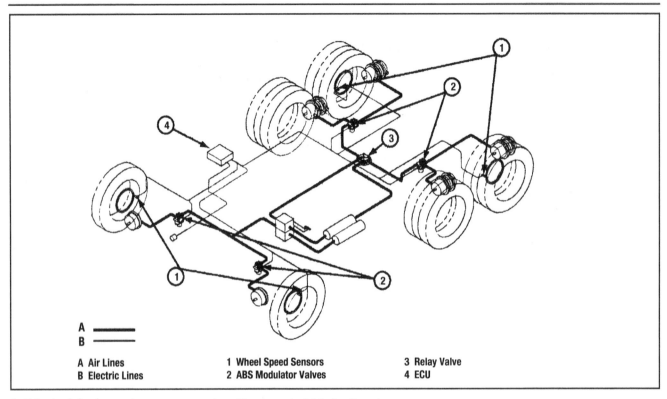

Anti-lock air brake system components. *(Courtesy: ArvinMeritor Corp.)*

A ———		
B ———		
A Air Lines	**1 Wheel Speed Sensors**	**3 Relay Valve**
B Electric Lines	**2 ABS Modulator Valves**	**4 ECU**

for powering trailer ABS
- Vehicles required to have an ABS also have a yellow ABS malfunction indicator light, which lights up to indicate most malfunctions
- The power unit's ABS malfunction light be 'in front of and in clear view' of the driver. It lights when the ignition key is first switched ON for a bulb check
- Air-braked tractors and trucks that tow other air-braked vehicles—built on or after March 1, 2001—have an in-cab warning light that indicates malfunctions in any towed trailer's or dolly's ABS. Its location and function are the same as for the powered unit's ABS malfunction light.
- Trucks required to have an ABS also have a yellow ABS malfunction indicator lamp, which lights up to indicate most malfunctions.
- The power unit's ABS malfunction lamp be 'in front of and in clear view' of the driver. It lights

when the ignition key is first switched ON for a bulb check.

Wheel speed data is sent to an electronic control unit (ECU). The ECU sends an electrical signal to solenoid valves, which modulate air pressure to the brake chamber(s) at the affected wheel(s). The new rate of deceleration is recognized by the ECU, which signals the solenoid valves to restore air pressure. This loop occurs multiple times per second, as long as the deceleration rate approaches lockup. This gives the driver the ability to maintain control of the vehicle during emergency braking situations.

Diagnosis

ABS systems all have some degree of self-diagnostic capability. For example, when a truck equipped with ABS is started, the system checks itself by cycling all valves and illuminating dash-mounted indicators. If everything checks okay, the lights go out once the truck starts rolling.

When a fault id detected in the ABS system, a fault code is stored in the ECU and the ABS indicator lamp illuminates. Thus, one basic step in troubleshooting ABS systems is reading the fault codes and interpreting what they mean.

The ECU stores two types of fault codes, inactive and active. Inactive codes describe malfunctions that may be intermittent. An intermittent code may be one that is set only when the vehicle is operated under certain conditions, such as when the vehicle is in motion, making turns, or travelling at a certain speed. Active codes are existing codes pertaining to a malfunction that happens all the time, no matter the conditions or driving speed. In either event, ECU trouble codes must be erased after the vehicle is repaired.

Remember, fault codes only point to the particular problem circuit. They don't necessarily tell you the exact component failure. Loose connections, broken wires, or improper peripheral component operation

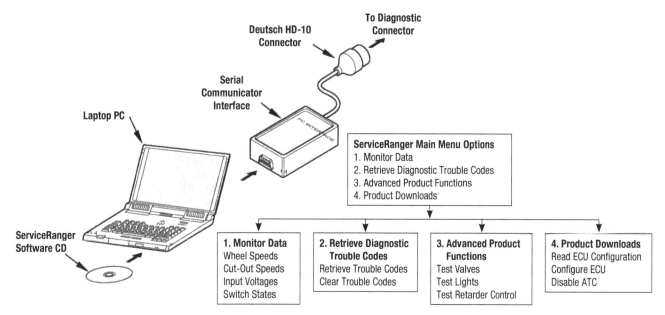

Using a laptop computer to diagnose an ABS system.   *(Courtesy: Eaton Corp.)*

could cause malfunctions, so give the ABS system a thorough visual inspection when diagnosing a malfunction.

Blink Code

The ABS indicator lamp, which is located on the dash, serves two purposes. First, it alerts the driver or technician to a possible fault in the ABS system. Secondly, it is capable of displaying diagnostic blink codes for easy servicing. Blink codes are a series of ABS indicator lamp flashes that will describe a particular condition in the ABS system.

On most trucks the code is retrieved by turning the ignition switch to the ON position, and activating the blink code switch. Then, the technician counts the ABS indicator lamp blinks to determine the particular malfunction. Most blink codes will indicate the type of system installed and the actual fault code. After the repair is made, perform the manufacturer's recommended procedure to erase the fault code.

Blink Code Switch

Check resistance between terminals while operating the switch, and check continuity of the wires to the switch from the electronic control unit.

Computer/Scan Tool

The system can also be tested by any number of commercially available computer programs or scan tools. With the ignition switch OFF, connect the computer or scan tool to the diagnostic port. This port is usually located under the left side dash panel, and requires a special connector made specifically for this purpose. Turn the computer or scan tool power on. Ensure that the blink code switch (if equipped) is in the off position, and make sure the computer or scan tool is configured in accordance with the specific ABS system. As faults are displayed, continue with the diagnostic process.

In addition, some programs may be equipped with service procedures, enabling the technician to diagnose and repair the system with an electronic repair manual.

Digital Multimeter

A digital multimeter can be used to check specific readings at critical component locations of the ABS system. The multimeter should be used in conjunction with blink codes to precisely isolate the specific problem.

Voltage Check

Voltage must be between 9.5 and 14 volts for the system to function properly. To check voltage, turn the ignition ON and connect a digital multimeter to the appropriate pins in the ECU. Consult the manufacturer's service manual for the specific pin location. If voltage is not up to specifications, check all wiring and connections before proceeding further.

Indicator Lamp

If the ABS indicator lamp does not light when the ignition is switched to the ON position, or it illuminates but does not go out after a brief (around 3 seconds) period of time, check all the ABS fuses or circuit breakers. Inspect wiring to the ABS diagnostic switch and the indicator lamp. Check the voltage potential at the lamp socket, continuity of the wires to the socket, and the bulb.

Component Removal And Installation

Wheel Speed Sensor

To check sensor output voltage, turn the ignition off and disconnect the electronic control unit. Raise and safely support the truck. Disconnect the sensor at its extension cable. Rotate the wheel and measure the voltage at the electronic control unit. Consult manufacturer's specification for the specific voltage range.

To check sensor resistance, turn the ignition off and disconnect the connector from the electronic control unit. Measure the output at the electronic control unit pins.

When replacing the wheel speed sensor, apply the parking brakes and block the wheels to prevent vehicle movement. Raise and safely support the vehicle, if necessary. If the wheel must be removed to gain access, release the parking brake and back off the slack adjuster to release the brake shoes.

Remove the wheel and tire assembly. Disconnect the sensor cable fasteners and disconnect the cable from the harness. Remove the sensor from its holder and twist the sensor to remove it from the sensor bracket, being careful not to pull on the sensor cable.

To install, connect the sensor cable to the wiring harness and install the fasteners. Apply suitable lubricant to the sensor and its spring clip. Install the clip and sensor assembly following manufacturer's recommendations.

Air Modulator

The air brake ABS modulator controls air pressure to each brake position during ABS application. To remove, completely depressurize the air brake system. Apply the parking brakes and block the front and rear wheels. Disconnect the harness connector from the modulator. Mark and remove the air lines from the modulator assembly. Remove the mounting screws and the modulator.

To install, position the modulator and bracket and install the mounting nuts. Connect and tighten the brake lines. Pressurize the system and check for operation and leakage.

HYDRAULICALLY OPERATED ABS

The National Highway Traffic Safety Administration (NHTSA) requires that ABS be installed on commercial trucks built (built meaning the official date of manufacture) on or after March 1, 1999, for hydraulically braked trucks and buses with gross vehicle weight ratings of more than 10,000 lbs.

There are three phases of hydraulic control that occur during an ABS stop. The first is called the pressure maintain phase. This means that any further brake fluid pressure to the slipping wheel or wheels is cut off.

Phase two is known as the pressure decrease function. If wheel slip continues to increase in the pressure maintain phase, hydraulic pressure to the wheel(s) is then decreased until wheel slip approaches zero. This means that wheel speed equals vehicle speed. At this point the pressure maintain phase is re-engaged.

The final phase is referred to as the pressure increase stage. If wheel slip approaches zero in the pressure maintain phase, hydraulic pressure to

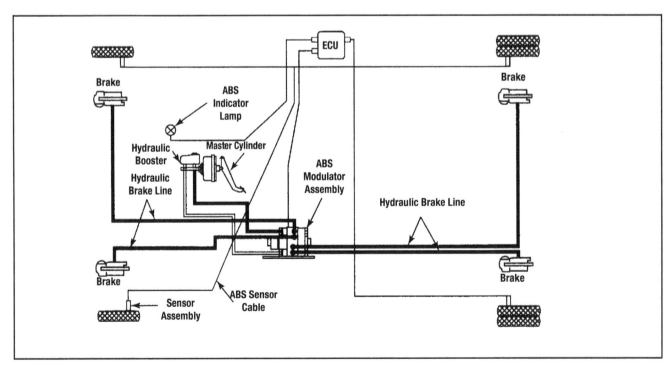

Hydraulic anti-lock brake system with frame-mounted electronic control unit. *(Courtesy: ArvinMeritor Corp.)*

the wheels(s) is increased until wheel slip begins to occur. This means that wheel speed is less than vehicle speed. The pressure increase phase is another name for normal brake operation, since maximum master cylinder pressure is applied to the wheels.

Component Removal And Installation

Wheel Speed Sensor

Apply the parking brakes and block the wheels to prevent vehicle movement. Raise and safely support the truck, if necessary. If the wheel must be removed to gain access, release the parking brake to release the brake shoes. Remove the wheel and tire assembly.

Disconnect the sensor cable fasteners and disconnect the cable from the harness. Remove the sensor from its holder and twist the sensor to remove it from the sensor bracket, being careful not to pull on the sensor cable.

To install, connect the sensor cable to the wiring harness and install the fasteners. Apply suitable lubricant to the sensor and its spring clip. Install the clip and sensor assembly following manufacturer's recommendations.

Hydraulic Modulator

Apply the parking brakes and block the front and rear wheels. Place a suitable container under the modulator to catch leaking brake fluid. Disconnect the harness connector from the modulator. Mark and remove the brake lines from the modulator assembly. Remove the mounting screws and the modulator.

To install, position the modulator and bracket and install the mounting nuts. Connect and tighten the brake lines. Bleed the brake system and connect the wiring harness.

Bleeding

Pressure Bleed

Always bleed the brake system in strict accordance with the manufacturer's service procedures. Apply the parking brakes and block the wheels to prevent vehicle movement. Make sure the ignition is off. Disconnect the battery cables.

NOTE: The ignition must remain off for the entire bleed procedure.

Fill a pressure bleeder with the appropriate brake fluid. Connect the pressure bleeder to the brake master cylinder. Set the pressure to 20-30 psi. Activate the bleed equipment and fill the master cylinder reservoir. Release the pressure for 3-5 seconds, and apply pressure for 10-15 seconds. Repeat these steps approximately 10 times before bleeding at the wheels. Next, set the filling pressure to 20-30 psi. Install a length of tubing to the bleeder fitting farthest away from the modulator.

Submerge the tubing in a suitable container of clean hydraulic brake fluid. Open the bleeder fitting until the fluid begins to flow. Allow fluid to flow until air is purged from the system. Repeat these steps to bleed the remaining brake actuators. Bleed

in the sequence of the longest to the shortest circuit from the modulator assembly.

Manual Bleed

Apply the parking brakes and block the wheels to prevent vehicle movement. Make sure the ignition is off. Disconnect the battery cables.

NOTE: The ignition must remain off for the entire bleed procedure.

Fill the master cylinder reservoir with the appropriate brake fluid. Depress the brake pedal five times using a stroke between 1/3 travel and maximum travel in five seconds. Release the pedal for 5-10 seconds. Repeat this procedure 3-4 times or until pedal resistance is felt. Install a length of tubing to the bleeder fitting farthest away from the modulator.

Submerge the tubing in a suitable container of clean hydraulic brake fluid. Have a helper depress the brake pedal 10-15 times and hold the pedal down after the last stroke. Open the bleeder fitting until the fluid begins to flow while the brake pedal travels through its maximum stroke. Tighten the fitting and repeat these steps to bleed the remaining brake actuators. Bleed in the sequence of the longest to the shortest

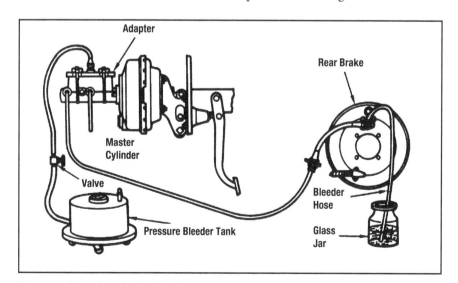

Pressure bleeding the hydraulic system.

circuit from the modulator assembly.

NOTE: Do not allow the hydraulic fluid in the master cylinder to drop below the minimum level during bleeding.

AUTOMATIC TRACTION CONTROL (ATC)

The ATC system works in tandem with the ABS system, utilizing wheel speed sensors and the ABS modulator. It consists of an ATC valve and an engine data transfer link to achieve traction control.

Connect a computer or scan tool to the diagnostic port and read the trouble codes. As with ABS, when a malfunction occurs in the ATC system, a fault code is stored in the ECU and the ATC indicator lamp illuminates. Active or inactive (sometimes both) codes can be stored in the ECU. Keep in mind that codes will only point to the problem circuit and loose connections, broken wires, or improper peripheral component operation could cause malfunctions.

As the antilock system helps control the truck during deceleration, automatic traction control helps to control the truck during acceleration. The traction control system will activate engine and/or brake control when the electronic control unit senses that the rotation of the driven wheels is higher than that of the non-driven wheels.

The brakes are controlled to prevent excess wheel spin by matching the rotation of the drive axle wheels with that of the non-drive axle wheels. When the wheel sensors send a signal to the electronic control unit that the wheel(s) are spinning faster than they should be, indicating a slip condition, engine control and/or brake control is activated.

The ATC function is enhanced by the fact that if the truck is on a surface with different road conditions on each side of the axle, the service brakes will be applied only at the slipping wheel, transferring torque to the wheel with greater traction. Therefore, ATC acts as an automatic differential lock to improve mobility and vehicle safety.

Engine control is achieved by communication from the electronic control unit of the ATC to the electronic control unit of the engine. When a wheel is excessively spinning, a signal is sent to the engine to limit its output torque via the SAE J1922, or J1939 power train data links.

ATC Control Valve Removal And Installation

Turn the ignition to the OFF position and apply the parking brakes. If necessary, raise and safely support the truck. Disconnect the wiring from the ATC valve. Relieve pressure by bleeding the air from the appropriate reservoir. Disconnect the supply and discharge lines of the valve. Remove the mounting screws/nuts and remove the valve.

To install, place the valve in position and secure with screws/ nuts. Connect the supply and discharge lines. Connect the ATC valve wiring, lower the truck and fully pressurize the air brake system. Check for proper operation.

ELECTRONIC STABILITY CONTROL (ESC)

It is a known fact that heavily loaded trucks are susceptible to a rollover accident when extreme maneuvers are made. The can potentially be disastrous due to weight transfer of cargo.

Electronic Stability Control (ESC) is designed to minimize the potential for a rollover. However, while ESC is designed to help with vehicle stability, it cannot override a truck's physical limits. The major difference between ESC and ABS or ATC is that ESC can be activated no matter what surface conditions exist, and has the capability of controlling the drivetrain in the event of an emergency. While ESC is integrated into the ABS system, it incorporates additional sensors for inputs such as steering wheel and gyroscopic (yaw) position.

Comparisons are made between the driver's steering and braking inputs and the truck's response to those inputs. When ESC senses an abnormal condition, such as an extreme lateral movement, it applies the brakes or reduces engine power. It works in conjunction with the ESC control module, microprocessors, yaw rate sensors, a vehicle acceleration sensor, steering angle sensor, and a lateral acceleration sensor. These sensors are strategically placed throughout the vehicle.

The yaw rate sensor provides a signal based on the direction change of the vehicle. Acceleration is determined by the vehicle acceleration (or wheel speed) sensor. The steering angle sensor informs the control module of the steering wheel position, and the lateral acceleration sensor provides a signal based on the lateral or side force on the vehicle through the curve.

Most ESC system problems are associated to signal loss due to sensor failures or wiring problems. However, failures in the ESC system can also be attributed to ABS or ATC system malfunctions.

Connect a computer or scan tool to the diagnostic port and read the trouble codes. As with ABS or ATC, when a malfunction occurs in the ESC system, a fault code is stored in the ECU and the ESC indicator lamp illuminates. Active or inactive (sometimes both) codes can be stored in the ECU. Keep in mind that codes will only point to the problem circuit and loose connections, broken wires, or improper peripheral component operation could cause malfunctions.

Prepare yourself for ASE testing with these questions on
MEDIUM/HEAVY-DUTY BRAKES

1. An air leak at point 'X' in the system shown above would cause which of these to leak down?
   A. #1 tank only
   B. #2 tank only
   C. #2 and #4 tanks only
   D. The entire system

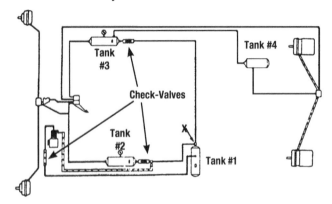

2. The Driver Vehicle Inspection Report (DVIR) should be submitted:
   A. according to the vehicle maintenance schedule
   B. when a failure occurs
   C. weekly
   D. daily

3. Which of the following cannot cause a drum on an air-braked vehicle to overheat?
   A. an over-tightened brake adjuster at that wheel
   B. under-adjusted brake(s) elsewhere on the vehicle
   C. too-high governor cut-out pressure
   D. driving downhill in too high a gear

4. All the brakes drag on a truck with hydraulic brakes. Which of the following could be the cause?
   A. air in the hydraulic system
   B. too high a vacuum supply to the power brake booster
   C. a leaking secondary cup in the master cylinder
   D. no brake pedal free travel

5. Which of the following could cause a pulsating brake pedal on a truck with hydraulic brakes?
   A. zero brake pedal free travel
   B. glazed linings
   C. an out-of-round brake drum
   D. a frozen wheel cylinder piston

6. Air pressure gauges change an air pressure signal into an electronic voltage signal using which of the following components?
   A. inductor
   B. capacitor
   C. transducer
   D. regulator

7. Technician A says that linings worn too thin on an air-braked vehicle can cause the S-camshaft to roll over. Technician B says this condition can cause excess brake pedal travel. Who is right?
   A. Technician A only
   B. Technician B only
   C. Both A and B
   D. Neither A or B

8. Spring brakes on an air-braked vehicle must be able to hold the vehicle facing uphill or downhill on what percent grade?
   A. 10%
   B. 20%
   C. 30%
   D. 40%

9. The driver of a truck with hydraulic brakes says the pedal reserve is too low. Technician A says the brakes could be out of adjustment. Technician B says one brake system may have failed. Who is right?
   A. Technician A only
   B. Technician B only
   C. Both A and B
   D. Neither A or B

10. The parking brakes fail to apply on a truck with air brakes. Technician A says this could be caused by low air pressure in the spring brake chamber. Technician B says this could be caused by a ruptured spring brake diaphragm. Who is right?
   A. Technician A only
   B. Technician B only
   C. Both A and B
   D. Neither A or B

11. Technician A says the low-pressure warning indicator is located on the secondary reservoir tank. Technician B says the low-pressure warning indicator operates once system air pressure falls below 80 psi. Who is right?

   A. Technician A

   B. Technician B

   C. Both A and B

   D. Neither A or B

12. The warning light on a truck with an anti-lock brake system lights when the truck is started. When the truck is moving, the light stays on. Which of the following could be the cause?

   A. misadjusted wheel sensor

   B. bad air release solenoid

   C. blown fail-safe monitor fuse

   D. bad warning light relay

13. The driver of a truck with air brakes says it has poor stopping power. Any of these could be the cause EXCEPT:

   A. The quick release valve exhaust port is plugged.

   B. The air pressure is too low.

   C. The service line is restricted.

   D. The brakes are adjusted incorrectly.

14. Technician A says brake shoe oil contamination should be no more than 10% of the lining surface. Technician B says oil contamination can lead to brake imbalance. Who is right?

   A. Technician A only

   B. Technician B only

   C. Both A and B

   D. Neither A or B

15. The driver of a truck with air brakes says that the brakes are slow to release. Which of the following is the LEAST likely cause?

   A. weak return springs

   B. a plugged exhaust port

   C. a kinked air line

   D. worn brake linings

16. An air-braked vehicle has lining wear tapered from inboard to outboard. There also is abrasion on the outer edges of the brake shoes. What could NOT be the cause?

   A. worn anchor pins

   B. worn outer S-cam bushings

   C. distorted anchor pin holes

   D. weak return springs

17. The low pressure warning light or buzzer activates at what pressure?

   A. 60 psi

   B. 70 psi

   C. 50 psi

   D. 40 psi

18. Normal governor cut-in pressure is set to what pressure?

   A. 150 psi

   B. 175 psi

   C. 125 psi

   D. 100 psi

19. When should the air tanks be drained on an air-braked vehicle with no air dryer.

   A. once a month

   B. once a week

   C. once a day

   D. never

20. Technician A says that low volume compressors are needed for applications such as trucks with multiple trailers. Technician B says that air compressors are available with up to four cylinders. Who is right?

   A. Technician A only

   B. Technician B only

   C. Both A and B

   D. Neither A or B

21. A technician has discovered oil in the brake reservoirs. Which of the following could be the cause?

   A. a clogged compressor air filter

   B. a leaking wheel seal

   C. a defective air tank pop off valve

   D. an incorrectly adjusted governor

22. A technician is rebuilding an air compressor. Before removing the connecting rod bolts, the technician should:
    A. lubricate the bearing caps and connecting rods
    B. mark the bearing caps and connecting rods
    C. check the cylinder walls for damage
    D. none of the above

23. Technician A says an air dryer has two cycles, charge and purge. Technician B says an air dryer collects moisture and contaminants before they get into the brake system. Who is right?
    A. Technician A only
    B. Technician B only
    C. Both A and B
    D. Neither A or B

24. The driver of an air-braked truck with ABS complains that on a panic stop in wet weather conditions, the truck's right rear wheel locks up. What could be the cause?
    A. a defective ABS/ECU
    B. an air leak in the primary reservoir
    C. a defective ABS wheel sensor
    D. a defective diagnostic switch

25. The driver of an air-braked truck complains that when he takes his foot off of the brake pedal to accelerate after a stop, the brakes do not release right away. What could be the cause?
    A. a defective pop off valve
    B. a defective quick release valve
    C. a defective tractor protection valve
    D. none of the above

26. What is the minimum allowable measurement for scoring of a brake drum?
    A. 0.020
    B. 0.010
    C. 0.10
    D. 0.21

27. Technician A says that a trailer control valve can be used to stop a moving combination vehicle. Technician B says that a trailer control valve is used to check the integrity of a fifth wheel connection. Who is right?
    A. Technician A only
    B. Technician B only
    C. Both A and B
    D. Neither A or B

28. A relay valve on trailer air brakes with too high of a crack pressure can cause:
    A. excessive brake wear
    B. premature brake application
    C. delayed brake application
    D. wheel lock-up

29. Technician A says disc brake rotor thickness must be measured in several places on the rotor using a dial indicator. Technician B says the thickness of disc brake rotors must not vary more than 0.005 in. Who is right?
    A. Technician A
    B. Technician B
    C. Both A and B
    D. Neither A or B

30. What causes the condition of 'brake fade?'
    A. brake linings get too hot
    B. hydraulic fluid contamination
    C. oil in the air system
    D. an air leak at the supply reservoir

31. The driver of a tractor/trailer combination with air brakes says that an air leak in the trailer system is causing the tractor brakes to lock up. Which of the following could be the cause?
    A. defective governor
    B. defective tractor protection valve
    C. clogged air compressor filter
    D. worn brake linings

32. The driver of a truck with hydraulic drum brakes complains that when his vehicle is unloaded, the rear brakes lock up on moderate to hard braking application. Which of the following could be the cause?
    A. defective metering valve
    B. leaking brake line
    C. defective proportioning valve
    D. brakes out of adjustment

33. Technician A says that Automatic Traction Control (ATC) controls the engine only. Technician B says that automatic traction control works in tandem with anti-lock brakes. Who is right?
 A. Technician A
 B. Technician B
 C. Both A and B
 D. Neither A or B

34. Proper voltage for an anti-lock brake system to function properly must be:
 A. 8.5 to 13 volts
 B. 12.0 to 18 volts
 C. 24.0 to 27 volts
 D. 9.5 to 14 volts

35. The driver of a truck with hydraulic power brakes complains of a hard brake pedal and poor stopping. Which of the following could be the cause?
 A. leaking master cylinder
 B. defective power brake booster
 C. defective proportioning valve
 D. leaking wheel cylinder

36. On a truck with air brakes, the air tank pop off valve releases air prematurely. A technician has removed and checked the valve and it has checked out OK. What else could cause this problem?
 A. governor adjustment
 B. kinked air hose
 C. defective drain valve
 D. defective pressure limiting valve

37. The minimum suggested lining thickness for drum brakes is:
 A. 1/2-in.
 B. 1/4-in
 C. 3/4-in.
 D. 1/3-in.

38. Technician A says that some compressor governors are adjustable. Technician B says that some governors are mounted in the engine compartment instead of on the compressor. Who is right?
 A. Technician A
 B. Technician B
 C. Both A and B
 D. Neither A or B

39. Technician A says that when both knobs on a dual circuit push-pull valve are pushed in, air is supplied to the tractor only. Technician B says that both knobs are pushed in to apply the parking brakes. Who is right?
 A. Technician A
 B. Technician B
 C. Both A and B
 D. Neither A or B

40. The driver of a truck with hydraulic disc/drum brakes says the truck dives when the brakes are applied. Which of the following could be the cause?
 A. defective metering valve
 B. defective proportioning valve
 C. defective safety valve
 D. defective check valve

41. A technician finds that during periods of low vacuum, a truck with hydraulic power brakes experiences a hard pedal when stopping. Which of the following could be the cause?
 A. defective one-way check valve
 B. leaking master cylinder
 C. improperly adjusted brakes
 D. crimped brake line

42. A truck with hydraulic brakes has developed a leak in the primary system, and the brake warning light is illuminated. What is the name of the switch that activates the dash light?
 A. warning differential switch
 B. metering differential switch
 C. backup relay switch
 D. pressure differential switch

43. Which of the following is NOT the name for a type of driveline parking brake?
 A. expanding disc
 B. contracting shoe
 C. expanding shoe
 D. disc

Prepare yourself for ASE testing with these questions on
MEDIUM/HEAVY-DUTY BRAKES

44. A driver complains of pulling to one side when the brakes are applied. A technician has physically checked the brakes and has found the system to be operating properly. What else should the technician check?
    A. axle seal leakage
    B. wheel bearing adjustment
    C. vehicle height
    D. coefficient of friction

45. Technician A says that DOT 3 brake fluid has a higher boiling point that DOT 4 brake fluid. Technician B says that DOT 5 brake fluid should not be used in a vehicle with ABS. Who is right?
    A. Technician A
    B. Technician B
    C. Both A and B
    D. Neither A or B

46. Technician A says that before a gear-driven air compressor is replaced, the gear must be timed with the engine prior to installation. Technician B says that when timing an air compressor gear, the piston in the engine's No. 1 cylinder must be at Top Dead Center. Who is right?
    A. Technician A
    B. Technician B
    C. Both A and B
    D. Neither A or B

47. A technician finds that an air-braked truck's service brakes grab or pull to one side when stopping. Which of the following could be the cause?
    A. glazed or contaminated lining
    B. insufficient air pressure
    C. overloaded vehicle
    D. defective quick-release valve

48. Technician A says automatic slack adjuster can be either stroke sensing or clearance sensing. Technician B says automatic slack adjusters can be adjusted during installation or in an emergency to move the vehicle. Who is right?
    A. Technician A
    B. Technician B
    C. Both A and B
    D. Neither A or B

49. A truck with a hydro-assist booster is experiencing a hard pedal. Which of the following could be the cause?
    A. low power steering pressure
    B. high brake fluid pressure
    C. high engine temperature
    D. leaking brake hose

50. When checking an application valve for internal leaks, an ultrasonic leak detector can be used at which port?
    A. exhaust port
    B. discharge port
    C. release port
    D. application port

51. All of the following are phases of hydraulic brake ABS control EXCEPT:
    A. pressure maintain
    B. pressure induction
    C. pressure increase
    D. pressure decrease

52. Technician A says that the driveline parking equalizes torque through the engine. Technician B says that the driveline parking brake is mounted on the rear of the transmission assembly. Who is right?
    A. Technician A
    B. Technician B
    C. Both A and B
    D. Neither A or B

53. When operating an air-braked vehicle at idle, air pressure should build from 85-100 psi in:
    A. 30 seconds
    B. 45 seconds
    C. 60 seconds
    D. 90 seconds

54. With foot pressure applied, the brake pedal on a truck with hydraulic power brakes moves down slightly when the engine is started. Technician A says that this condition can be caused by a leaking power brake booster diaphragm. Technician B says that the cause could be a faulty power brake booster check valve. Who is right?
    A. Technician A
    B. Technician B
    C. Both A and B
    D. Neither A or B

Prepare yourself for ASE testing with these questions on
MEDIUM/HEAVY-DUTY BRAKES

55. Technician A says a 4-channel ABS system independently controls all of the brakes on a 3-axle vehicle. Technician B says a 6-channel system is needed to independently control all of the brakes on a 3-axle vehicle. Who is right?
   A. Technician A
   B. Technician B
   C. Both A and B
   D. Neither A or B

56. Hydraulic brakes that drag or fail to release can be caused by which component in the master cylinder.
   A. leaking primary cup
   B. leaking secondary cup
   C. failure of the residual pressure check valve
   D. clogged compensating port

57. Technician A says that a stoplight switch on a truck with air brakes operates electro-pneumatically in tandem with a two-way check valve. Technician B says that a failure in the stoplight switch causes the trailer control valve to activate. Who is right?
   A. Technician A
   B. Technician B
   C. Both A and B
   D. Neither A or B

58. All of the following names describe air brake reservoirs EXCEPT:
   A. primary
   B. secondary
   C. auxiliary
   D. supply

59. Technician A says that the pressure side of the turbocharger supplies air to the air compressor. Technician B says that air can be drawn into the compressor from the atmosphere. Who is right?
   A. Technician A
   B. Technician B
   C. Both A and B
   D. Neither A or B

60. The oil in an air compressor with its own sump should be checked:
   A. once a week
   B. every two weeks
   C. once a month
   D. once a day

61. Technician A says the brake ABS is used to control the truck during deceleration. Technician B says ATC is used to keep loads from shifting. Who is right?
   A. Technician A
   B. Technician B
   C. Both A and B
   D. Neither A or B

62. Technician A says automatic slack adjusters improve brake balance and reduce downtime and maintenance costs. Technician B says manual slack adjusters provide reduced chamber travel and less air consumption. Who is right?
   A. Technician A
   B. Technician B
   C. Both A and B
   D. Neither A or B

63. A slack adjuster essentially functions as a:
   A. gear
   B. lever
   C. anchor
   D. servo

64. Technician A says coefficient of friction is the amount of heat absorbed into the drum. Technician B says brake shoes with high coefficient of friction will slow a truck with less application pressure. Who is right?
   A. Technician A
   B. Technician B
   C. Both A and B
   D. Neither A or B

65. Air disc brakes are designed to:
   A. apply faster
   B. last longer
   C. decrease in-lane braking stability
   D. none of the above

66. The right front wheel of a truck with hydraulic anti-lock brakes locks up when on a slippery surface. Technician A says the truck could have a defective wheel sensor. Technician B says the sensor checks for a lock-up condition and sends a signal to the hydraulic modulator. Who is right?
    A. Technician A
    B. Technician B
    C. Both A and B
    D. Neither A or B

67. New generation ABS systems are designed to:
    A. allow the driver to apply with more foot pressure
    B. allow the pedal to be pumped
    C. default to non-ABS when a failure is detected
    D. none of the above

68. A truck with air brakes takes an inordinate time to build up adequate air pressure. Oil has been found in the air brake system. Technician A says the compressor air filter could be clogged. Technician B says the compressor oil control rings could be worn. Who is right?
    A. Technician A
    B. Technician B
    C. Both A and B
    D. Neither A or B

69. Electronic Stability Control (ESC) is designed to:
    A. warn the driver if the brakes have failed
    B. establish communication between the tractor and trailer
    C. activate the hydro-boost system
    D. sense abnormal steering and braking

70. When a truck is pulling to one side when braking, it could have:
    A. impractical imbalance
    B. mechanical imbalance
    C. braking instability
    D. adaptive coefficiency

71. Technician A says most manufacturers recommend checking automatic slack adjuster internal clutch operation with a torque wrench. Technician B says if the free stroke is within manufacturer's specifications, but the applied stroke is not, the problem could be with the automatic slack adjuster. Who is right?
    A. Technician A
    B. Technician B
    C. Both A and B
    D. Neither A or B

72. Technician A says it is acceptable to repair a leaking brake line by replacing only the leaking section. Technician B says a soft brake hose can be a symptom of an internal collapse. Who is right?
    A. Technician A
    B. Technician B
    C. Both A and B
    D. Neither A or B

73. Technician A says active ABS fault codes are intermittent. Technician B says fault codes explain the exact component failure. Who is right?
    A. Technician A
    B. Technician B
    C. Both A and B
    D. Neither A or B

74. Which of the following best describes the operation of an air-operated ABS system?
    A. works in tandem with ATC
    B. operates differently than a hydraulic ABS system
    C. monitors engine acceleration
    D. minimizes potential for rollover

75. Blue marks on a disc brake rotor indicate which of the following:
    A. excessive heat
    B. identification marks
    C. resurfacing specifications
    D. excessive cooling

Notes

Answers to Study-Guide Test Questions

1. The correct answer is A. If you look closely at the diagram, you will notice two check-valves at tanks 2 and 3. An air leak at the point indicated would be isolated to tank 1 only; therefore only tank 1 would lose air pressure in the circuit.

2. The correct answer is D. Federal Motor Vehicle Safety Standards (FMVSS) require the driver to submit a DVIR to their motor carrier or owner at the end of each day. The DVIR is used to identify defects or deficiencies that would result in a mechanical breakdown or effect the safe operation of a vehicle. Once a driver submits the DVIR, a motor carrier or its agent must investigate and repair the defect or deficiency.

3. The correct answer is C. The governor controls the air compressor output by unloading or cycling it. It has no direct effect on the mechanical brake parts. While the pressure setting is important to maintain air brake system pressure within acceptable limits, an incorrect setting will not cause the drum on an air-braked vehicle to overheat. All other choices given, however, will cause overheating problems.

4. The correct answer is D. Only a brake pedal with no free travel will cause all of the brakes to drag. Answer A–air in the hydraulic system, will cause a spongy pedal, while answer B–too high a vacuum to the power booster, won't affect brake drag at all. Answer C, a leaking secondary cup in the master cylinder, could increase pedal travel, but won't cause the brakes to drag.

5. The correct answer is C. Of the choices given, only an out-of-round brake drum can cause pulsation in a hydraulic brake system. Answer A, zero brake pedal free travel, will cause a dragging brake condition, but not pulsation. Answer B, glazed linings, will affect stopping performance and noise, and answer D, a frozen wheel cylinder, will degrade stopping performance, but will not cause pulsation.

6. The correct answer is C. An element inside an air pressure transducer responds to air pressure increase or decrease, and the transducer converts that pressure differentiation into a voltage signal, which is displayed in a proportionate reading on the dash gauge.

7. The correct answer is A. The brake adjuster is connected to a shaft that runs perpendicular to the plane formed by the pushrod and slack adjuster. As the pushrod is extended, the shaft rotates. The shaft, in turn, is connected to an S-shaped cam between the brake shoes. As the shaft rotates, so does the cam. The brake shoes are forced apart and against the brake drum, creating the friction needed to slow the vehicle. Thin brake linings can allow the S-cam to roll over, but will not affect brake pedal travel.

8. The correct answer is B. Per Federal Motor Vehicle Safety Standard (FMVSS) 121, the parking brakes must be able to hold a vehicle, loaded to its gross weight rating, stationary on a smooth, dry, concrete roadway, facing uphill or downhill on a 20% grade. In the emergency mode, the parking brakes must be able to exert a retarding force equal to 28% of the gross axle rating.

9. The correct answer is C, both Technicians are right. Either condition will cause the driver to notice a low pedal reserve.

10. The correct answer is D, neither technician is right. In addition to applying the service brakes used in everyday driving, the brake chambers on the rear tractor axles and on the trailer axles apply the parking brakes. These brake chambers (spring brakes) incorporate a second chamber containing a second diaphragm and a powerful spring. When the vehicle is in use, air pressure supplied to the spring diaphragm compresses the spring and the parking brakes are held off. When the vehicle is parked, the dash valves are pulled out. This exhausts spring brake hold-off air, allowing the spring to apply the parking brakes. Neither low air pressure in the spring brake chamber nor a ruptured diaphragm can prevent the parking brake from being applied.

11. The correct answer is D, neither technician. The low-pressure warning indicator is installed in the primary reservoir tank, and notifies the operator of system air depletion when the pressure falls below 60 psi.

12. The correct answer is A. When a vehicle equipped with ABS is started, the system checks itself by cycling all valves and illuminating dash-mounted indicator lights. If everything checks OK, the lights go out once the vehicle starts rolling. In the event of a fault, one indicator light stays on, and the affected part of the system reverts to conven-

Answers to Study-Guide Test Questions

tional brake system operation. A specialized tester is then used to pinpoint the problem. In this case, however, the only possible cause would be a misadjusted wheel sensor, because the blown fuse (answer C) or bad relay (answer D) wouldn't allow the warning light to illuminate at all, and answer B, a bad air release solenoid wouldn't be detected since it's not wired into the electronic diagnostic system.

13. The correct answer is A. The quick release valve operates to release the brakes; all other choices indicate functions that serve to apply the brakes. Low air pressure, a restricted service line or misadjusted brakes can cause poor stopping power.

14. The correct answer is C. If the lining is otherwise okay, but an area no larger than 10 percent of the total lining area is contaminated by grease or oil, the spot can be cleaned with brake cleaning solvent (not gasoline or another substitute). However, this isn't the safest option, as it could lead to a brake imbalance condition if done improperly.

15. The correct answer is D. Of the choices given, only worn brake linings would not cause slow brake release. Weak return springs, a plugged exhaust port or a kinked air line all could result in a slow brake release condition.

16. The correct answer is D. Lining wear should be even around the circumference of the brake assembly, and from inboard to outboard. More wear on the bottom, top or one side could indicate that peripheral brake hardware is worn. Worn anchor pins, holes and bushings, or outer S-cam bushings can allow applied force to push the shoes to one side, resulting in tapered lining wear. This condition often is accompanied by outer-edge abrasion on the shoes, caused by the shoes tracking out of alignment due to worn parts.

17. The correct answer is A. The low pressure warning indicator is installed on the primary reservoir, and notifies the operator of system air depletion by sounding a warning buzzer, and in some cases, illuminating a light on the instrument panel, when pressure drops to approximately 60 psi.

18. The correct answer is D. On a typical system, when the air pressure in the supply reservoir falls below 100 psi, the governor 'cuts in' and signals the compressor to

deliver air to the reservoirs. The governor regulates the air compressor's output and keeps it from over-supplying the system with an excessive amount of air pressure.

19. The correct answer is C. Manual valves should be drained on a daily basis, especially in humid or wet climates where excessive amounts of moisture are present. Drain valves are installed in each reservoir to help purge the system from its worst enemy, moisture.

20. The correct answer is B. A single-cylinder or two-cylinder compressor is used for most truck applications. However, three- and four-cylinder air compressors are available for applications where high air volume is in demand, such as on trucks with multiple trailers and air-powered accessories.

21. The correct answer is A. In addition to a slow air compressor build-up time, a clogged filter creates a vacuum in the compressor cylinder during the intake stroke. Oil is then sucked past the compressor's piston rings. On the compression stroke, the piston pumps all of the accumulated oil through the discharge line, and right into the air system. Oil in the air system can gum up major components, causing them to fail prematurely.

22. The correct answer is B. Before the connecting rod bolts are removed, each connecting rod and bearing cap must be marked. The connecting rod and its corresponding cap must be matched together upon reassembly.

23. The correct answer is C. The air dryer removes moisture and contaminants from the air system before the compressed air travels to the primary reservoir. The air dryer operates in two cycles, charge and purge. The charge cycle accepts compressed air, sometimes contaminated with moisture or debris, from the air compressor. Compressed air travels through an oil separator where oil and solid contaminants are removed. Water, and water vapor is removed from the air by way of desiccant material. The air then enters the primary tank through a one-way check valve. Once the governor cut-out pressure is achieved, the governor signals the air dryer to begin the purge cycle. This signal opens the purge port of the air dryer to allow contaminants to exit through to the atmosphere. The valve stays open until the governor cut-in pressure is achieved, signaling the compressor to once again build air pressure.

Answers to Study-Guide Test Questions

24. The correct answer is C. Each sensor/wheel combination is a kind of electric generator consisting of a permanent magnet and coil. As the rotating teeth pass a sensor, the magnetic flux picked up by the coil is intermittently altered. Alternating voltage is produced, the strength and frequency of which are proportional to wheel speed. Wheel speed data is sent to an Electronic Control Unit (ECU), which sends an electrical signal to solenoid valves that reduce air pressure to the brake chamber(s) at the affected wheel(s). The new rate of deceleration is recognized by the ECU, which signals the solenoid valves to restore air pressure. This loop occurs repeatedly, as long as the deceleration rate approaches lock-up.

25. The correct answer is B. After a stop, when the driver lifts his foot from the brake pedal, a quick release valve allows brake actuation air to be quickly exhausted near the brakes it serves, rather than having to travel back through the supply line, thus speeding brake release time.

26. The correct answer is B. Light scoring should be no deeper than 0.010-in. It is permissible to resurface a drum to 0.060-in. oversize, but bear in mind that the radius of the new lining will not match that of the drum. Reduced braking performance and lining damage can result.

27. The correct answer is B. The primary function of the trailer control valve is to allow the operator to check the fifth wheel connection by attempting to move the coupled vehicle with the trailer brakes applied. Because of its graduated application, some drivers use the trailer control valve by applying it while the combination is in motion to save wear and tear on the tractor brakes. This practice is not recommended and is in some cases hazardous, causing trailer sway while driving, and contributing to accelerated wear of the trailer brakes.

28. The correct answer is C. Crack pressure that is too high can cause delayed application, insufficient braking and trailer pushing, if the affected axle is on the trailer.

29. The correct answer is B. A micrometer, not a dial indicator is used to measure the thickness of a rotor in several places around its circumference. The rotor must be discarded if the measurement is less than 0.040 over the minimum manufacturer's specified thickness, or if the measurements vary more than 0.005-in.

30. The correct answer is A. Brake fade is a condition of brake lining overheating. When fade occurs, lining-to-drum friction is reduced and vehicle stopping distance is increased. Different linings have different fade characteristics. Therefore, if mismatched linings are installed on different axles, brake action and balance are affected.

31. The correct answer is B. A tractor protection valve senses pressure in one or both lines that carry air to the trailer. These lines are connected to the trailer by means of quick-connect air fittings called 'gladhands.' When there is no pressure in the line(s) due to trailer break-away or a gross air leak in the trailer circuit, the valve closes to maintain air pressure in the tractor circuit. In everyday use, the valve also works in conjunction with the dash-mounted trailer parking brake valve to shut off air to the trailer circuit before disconnecting the tractor from the trailer.

32. The correct answer is C. A defective or leaking load proportioning valve will cause rear brake lock-up during moderate to hard brake application, brake drag, grabbing, and premature rear brake wear.

33. The correct answer is B. The ATC system works in tandem with the ABS system, utilizing wheel speed sensors and the ABS modulator. It consists of an ATC valve and an engine data transfer link to achieve traction control. The ATC system will activate engine and/or brake control when the electronic control unit senses that the rotation of the driven wheels is higher than that of the non-driven wheels.

34. The correct answer is D. Voltage must be between 9.5 and 14 volts for the system to function properly. To check voltage, turn the ignition on and connect a volt/ohmmeter to the proper pins in the electronic control unit. Consult the manufacturer's service manual for the specific pin locations.

35. The correct answer is B. A defective brake booster would not perform the assist function, causing a hard brake pedal. When the brake pedal is pushed, atmospheric pressure is introduced into the chamber on the firewall side of the brake booster diaphragm. This action causes a pressure differential, forcing the booster power piston forward, actuating the master cylinder.

Answers to Study-Guide Test Questions

36. The correct answer is D. The pressure limiting (or proportioning) valve reduces pressure to components that do not necessarily need full system pressure such as air suspensions, tank vents and drains.

37. The correct answer is B. Replace the linings if unusually patterned cracks are found and the lining measures less than 1/4-in. at its lowest point.

38. The correct answer is C. The governor may be attached to the compressor or externally mounted in the engine compartment with a line connected to it from the compressor. The governor is adjustable if an adjustment screw is present, and the cover is not marked non-adjustable. Take caution not to over adjust the governor. Each 1/4 turn of the adjustment screw can raise or lower the pressure settings approximately 4 psi.

39. The correct answer is D. The dual unit controls the parking brakes on the tractor and the air supply on the trailer. When both valves are in, air is supplied to the tractor and trailer spring brake chambers to release the parking brakes.

40. The correct answer is A. A brake metering valve is used on front disc/rear drum brake systems for the purpose of providing simultaneous application of all brakes. The valve is located in the front brake hydraulic circuit, and delays front brake operation until the rear brakes begin to operate. When the rear brakes make contact with the drums, hydraulic pressure in the front circuit will open the metering valve, sending pressurized fluid to the front brakes.

41. The correct answer is A. The one-way check valve is designed to maintain brake assist during periods of low vacuum. The booster is connected to intake manifold vacuum on gasoline engines, or to a vacuum pump on diesel engines, by way of a vacuum hose and one-way check valve.

42. The correct answer is D. The pressure differential warning switch illuminates a warning light to alert the driver of pressure loss in one of the hydraulic circuits. Under normal operating conditions, the hydraulic pressure on both sides of the pressure differential piston is balanced and the piston is centered. In this position, a spring-loaded plunger opens the contacts and keeps the brake warning light off. If one of the circuits develops a leak, the higher pressure in the other circuit will move the piston to one side. This causes the pressure differential switch to close, completing the circuit and illuminating the brake warning light.

43. The correct answer is A. The correct names of the different types of driveline parking brakes are Contracting Shoe, which squeezes the outer portion of the driveline parking brake drum, Expanding Shoe, which expands into the driveline parking brake drum, and Disc, which squeezes a disc brake rotor assembly in order for the parking brakes to hold.

44. The correct answer is B. In addition to malfunctioning brake system parts, worn out hubs and wheel bearings can also contribute to poor braking performance. Many apparent braking problems that persist after all the worn brake parts have been replaced can actually be caused by wheel bearings being worn out or misadjusted.

45. The correct answer is B. Since DOT 5 brake fluid is silicone based, it's prone to aeration. This means that when the fluid is agitated, tiny air bubbles, like those found in a carbonated drink, form in the fluid. For this reason, DOT 5 brake fluid should never be used in an anti-lock brake system. The boiling point of DOT 3 is lower (401°F) than that of DOT 4 brake fluid (446°F).

46. The correct answer is C. If the compressor is gear-driven, the drive gear must be meshed with the timing gear on the engine prior to installation. A misaligned compressor drive gear can cause poor compressor air build up. On most engines, compressor timing is achieved by aligning the timing marks on the compressor drive gear and crankcase. The engine's No. 1 cylinder must be brought to Top Dead Center (TDC), and the air compressor drive gear must be aligned.

47. The correct answer is A. Glazed or contaminated linings would cause the vehicle to pull to one side when braking, especially on the front axle. The lining should also be checked for foreign material that may be imbedded. If linings are contaminated with oil or grease, correct the cause before re-lining. The problem is almost always a leaking oil seal, too much grease on a grease-type wheel bearing or camshaft bushing, or the result of careless handling.

48. The correct answer is C, both technicians. Automatic slack adjusters come in two variations; stroke sensing and clearance sensing. Stroke sensing slack adjusters

Answers to Study-Guide Test Questions

are designed to react to the amount of brake chamber push rod travel. If the travel is past a pre-determined limit, the unit will adjust the brakes accordingly. Clearance sensing slack adjusters are designed to sense the lining-to-drum clearance and adjust when the brakes are released. The National Transportation Safety Board (NTSB) has recommended not to adjust automatic slack adjusters except during installation or in an emergency to move the vehicle to a repair facility.

49. The correct answer is A. The hydro-boost system is a variation on the conventional vacuum-assist system. It operates by using the power steering pump fluid pressure instead of manifold vacuum.

50. The correct answer is A. An ultrasonic leak detector can be used at the exhaust port to detect internal air leaks. The tool transposes the sound of an air leak, no matter how small, into a frequency that can be heard through headphones. Also, the intensity of the signal can be observed on an LCD display. In all other cases, soapy water can be used.

51. The correct answer is B. The three phases of hydraulic control that occur during an ABS stop are pressure maintain, pressure decrease, and pressure increase. Pressure maintain means that any further brake fluid pressure to the slipping wheel or wheels is cut off. Phase two is known as the pressure decrease function. If wheel slip continues to increase in the pressure maintain phase, hydraulic pressure to the wheel(s) is then decreased until wheel slip approached zero. This means that wheel speed equals vehicle speed. At this point the pressure maintain phase is re-engaged. The final phase is referred to as the pressure increase stage. If wheel slip approaches zero in the pressure maintain phase, hydraulic pressure to the wheel(s) is increased until wheel slip begins to occur. This means that wheel speed is less than vehicle speed. The pressure increase phase is another name for normal brake operation, since maximum master cylinder pressure is applied to the wheels.

52. The correct answer is B. The driveline parking brake is mounted at the rear of the transmission. While the operation of these brakes varies, the basic principles are the same. The braking mechanism, mounted on the rear of the transmission or transfer case, holds the vehicle by equalizing torque through the differential.

53. The correct answer is B. With the engine running at idle, air pressure should build from 85-100 psi (pounds per square inch) within 45 seconds. If the engine is running at full-governed rpm, air should build up within 25 seconds, and the compressor should maintain a constant pressure of 100-120 psi.

54. The correct answer is D, neither Technician is right. With the brake pedal applied while starting the engine, the pedal should move down slightly, indicating that the vacuum booster is operating properly.

55. The correct answer is B. The number of channels in an individual-wheel control system refers to the number of individual brakes its ECU is capable of independently controlling. For example, a system that can independently accommodate all of the brakes on a steer axle and tandem is referred to as a 6-channel system. A 4-channel system can also be applied to a 3-axle vehicle, but the front and rear wheels on either side of the tandem would be braked simultaneously, rather than independently.

56. The correct answer is D. The compensating port allows for residual hydraulic line pressure to be discharged into the reservoir as the brake pedal is released. A clogged or restricted compensating port will create a pressure build-up, which will cause the brakes to drag or fail to release. The cup can be clogged by foreign matter, blocked by a swollen primary cup or covered by the primary cup if the master cylinder pushrod is improperly adjusted.

57. The correct answer is A. The stoplight switch is an electro-pneumatic, non-grounded switch that operates in tandem with a two-way check valve. When the brakes are applied, the air pressure moves an internal switch that completes the circuit, lighting the stoplights. A defective stoplight switch will not cause the trailer control valve to actuate.

58. The correct answer is C. The supply reservoir feeds air to the primary and secondary reservoirs of the split service system. When the brake pedal is depressed, air flows from the primary reservoir, through the primary section of the foot valve, and out to the rear foundation brakes. Meanwhile, at the same time, air flows from the secondary reservoir through the secondary section of the foot valve to actuate the front foundation brakes.

Answers to Study-Guide Test Questions

59. The correct answer is C. Air can be drawn into the compressor directly from the atmosphere through a filter, or from the pressure side of the engine turbocharger. When the air enters the compressor cylinder, it is compressed by the upward motion of the piston, and forced through a discharge valve to the supply reservoir.

60. The correct answer is D. Some air compressors utilize their own oil sumps. If the compressor is self-lubricated, the oil should be checked daily. If oil is pumped in from the engine compartment, the engine oil should be checked in accordance with the engine manufacturer's scheduled maintenance intervals.

61. The correct answer is A. The Anti-lock Brake System (ABS) helps control the truck during deceleration. Automatic Traction Control (ATC) helps to control the truck during acceleration.

62. The correct answer is A. Having the slack adjusters automatically adjust alleviates the need for the driver or technician to adjust them. The result is reduced down time and less maintenance. Also, automatic slack adjusters will maintain brake balance, minimize travel and lessen air consumption. Manual slack adjusters must be constantly adjusted for minimal travel and reduced air consumption.

63. The correct answer is B. The slack adjuster is essentially a lever, which multiplies force in proportion to its length. The brake adjuster's length and the brake chamber's size are two variables commonly altered to meet braking requirements.

64. The correct answer is B. Coefficient of friction is defined as the resistance to movement between two surfaces in contact with each other. The amount of such resistance is known as the coefficient of friction (sometimes represented by the Greek letter 'μ,' pronounced 'mew'). Lining with a high coefficient of friction would slow a truck with less application pressure than a lining having a lower coefficient of friction.

65. The correct answer is D. Air disc brake technology improves in-lane braking stability as compared to S-Cam brakes. Small variations in lining friction or the drum surface on S-cam brakes can affect braking stability. Air disc brakes are designed to minimize this instability as pressure is applied constantly and efficiently to all wheels.

66. The correct answer is C, both Technicians are right. Hydraulic anti-lock systems use a control module in conjunction with wheel speed sensors to establish the deceleration rate of the vehicle's wheels during braking. If the control module determines that wheel lock-up is about to take place, it will issue commands to a hydraulic modulator. The modulator will then regulate fluid pressure to the wheels as instructed.

67. The correct answer is C. All new-generation anti-lock systems are designed to default to what is typically called a 'fail soft' condition—that is, when there is an ABS malfunction, the brake system simply behaves as though there was no ABS.

68. The correct answer is C, both Technicians are right. In addition to a slow air compressor build-up time, a plugged filter creates a vacuum in the compressor cylinder during the intake stroke. Oil is then sucked past the compressor's piston rings. On the compression stroke, the piston pumps all of the accumulated oil through the discharge line, and right into the air system. A compressor can also pass oil into the system if its oil control rings are excessively worn.

69. The correct answer is D. ESC systems are integrated into the ABS and activate in situations where vehicle stability is crucial. Comparisons are made between the truck driver's steering and braking inputs and the truck's response to those inputs. When ESC senses an abnormal condition such as an extreme lateral movement, it applies the brakes or reduces engine power.

70. The correct answer is B. If the vehicle's brakes are pulling to one side, grabbing too quickly, improperly releasing, or otherwise causing the vehicle to experience poor stopping ability, the system could be experiencing what is called 'mechanical imbalance.'

71. The correct answer is A. Most manufacturers recommend checking the slack adjuster internal clutch operation using a torque wrench. If the automatic slack adjuster free stroke is within manufacturer's specifications, but the applied stroke is not, suspect a problem with the foundation brakes. If both the free stroke and applied stroke are out of specification, suspect either a foundation brake or automatic slack adjuster problem.

72. The correct answer is B. It is not recommended, and in most cases, illegal to splice a leaking brake line. Lines must be replaced with DOT approved material intended for the specific application. While the outside of the hose may look acceptable, the inside may be collapsed to the point that it will not allow the proper amount of brake fluid to the brake components.

73. The correct answer is D, neither technician. The ECU stores two types of fault codes, active and inactive. Active codes are existing codes pertaining to a malfunction that happens all the time, no matter the conditions or driving speed. Inactive codes describe malfunctions that may be intermittent. Fault codes only point to the particular problem circuit. They don't necessarily tell you the exact component failure.

74. The correct answer is A. The ATC system works in tandem with the ABS system, utilizing wheel speed sensors and the ABS modulator. It consists of an ATC valve and an engine data transfer link to achieve traction control. Air operated antilock brakes operate similarly to hydraulic antilock brakes. Engine acceleration and rollover protection are functions of ESC.

75. The correct answer is A. Blue discoloration indicates a change in the internal crystalline structure of the metal. The rotor at one time was excessively hot, probably due to a malfunction in the brake system.

Notes

Notes

Glossary of Terms

--a--

ABA - automatic brake adjuster (see automatic slack adjuster). A lever connecting the brake chamber pushrod with the foundation brake camshaft. It provides torque to rotate the brake camshaft when the brake treadle is depressed. It also provides a means of adjusting clearance between brake shoes and the drum to compensate for lining wear.

abrasion - rubbing away or wearing of a component.

abrasive cleaning - removing contaminants using a cleaning agent containing abrasive material. Cleaning that requires physical abrasion (e.g., glass bead blasting, wire brushing).

ABS - abbreviation for 'anti-lock brake system.' ABS electronically monitors wheel speed and prevents wheel lock-up by rapidly cycling the brakes during panic stops and when stopping on low-friction surfaces.

ABS control valves - control valves that are actuated by the ABS electronic control unit (ECU) to ensure wheels are optimally braked. On a tractor, they are called ABS modulator valves. On a trailer, they're called ABS relay valves.

absorb - to trap liquids or gases with an absorbent material.

accumulator - in a non-integral ABS system, a chamber that temporarily stores fluid during the pressure decrease phase of ABS operation; in an integral ABS system, a sealed vessel containing a thick flexible diaphragm that separates brake fluid from high-pressure nitrogen gas.

actuate - to initiate mechanical motion of a brake system component.

actuator - a device that physically initiates the mechanical motion of a brake system component.

aeration - to expose to the air or mix with air, as with a liquid; to charge a liquid with gas.

aftercooler - optional device that condenses and eliminates water from air that has been pressurized by the compressor.

aftermarket - parts and equipment manufacturing that is not original equipment from the factory.

air build-up - the process of compressor-building (increasing) pressure to a predetermined maximum level (usually 100-120 psi) within the brake system air tanks.

air compressor - engine-driven via a belt or direct gear, the compressor pressurizes the air tanks.

air compressor cut-out - predetermined point at which the air governor halts compression of air by the compressor.

air disc brakes - air-actuated brakes that, upon application, employ a caliper to clamp two brake pads against a rotor. Air discs, compared with drum-type brakes, are better able to resist fade.

air dryer - a filter, typically containing a desiccant, which is installed between the compressor and service reservoir to remove water and vapor plus oil blow-by from the compressor.

air gauge - dash-mounted gauge indicating air pressure in terms of pounds per square inch (psi).

air governor - controls the compressor unloader mechanism and also maintains system air pressure between predetermined minimum and maximum levels (usually, between 90-120 psi).

air hose - line in which air is supplied to various points throughout a vehicle.

air tank - reservoir for compressed air. Typically, a combination vehicle has several tanks—three in the tractor and two per trailer. The tractor's supply air tank (formerly wet tank) receives air from the compressor and delivers it to the primary and secondary air tanks in the tractor. Most trailers also have primary and secondary tanks. A check-valve on each tank prevents total air loss in the event of a leak.

air tank bleeder - valve used to expel air and contaminants from the air tank in order to maintain an efficient air system.

alcohol evaporator - optional device, installed in compressor discharge line between the compressor and supply air tank, which injects alcohol mist into the air flow to reduce the risk of freeze-up. It's not normally used in a vehicle with an air dryer.

American Trucking Associations (ATA) - organization formed to advance the trucking industry's image, efficiency, competitiveness and profitability; to provide educational programs and industry research; and to promote highway and driver safety.

Glossary of Terms

analog processing - a method of processing information used in older ABS control units. Today's electronic control units (ECUs) use digital processing, which is many times faster and more reliable.

anchor pin - a pin or pins used to retain brake shoes within the brake assembly.

anti-compounding - basically, an optional system that prevents application of service brakes from compounding (adding to) the force exerted by parking brakes. Functionally, this guards against brake cracking and lining damage.

antilock brake system (ABS) - computer controlled system that allows the vehicle to be controlled under heavy braking by releasing pressure to wheels that are about to lock up and skid. Sensors located at the wheels, monitor rotating wheel speed in relation to other wheels and send the information to a control module that in turn controls a modulator, which regulates pressure to each brake assembly.

anti-rattle spring - device used with disc brake pads to keep them from moving and making noise.

application time - time elapsed between depression of the brake treadle and engagement of the linings with the drums (or per FMVSS 121, the point at which all service chambers reach 60 psi).

application valve - air valve, such as foot valve or trailer control valve, which controls the pressure delivered to brake chambers.

ASE - see National Institute for Automotive Service Excellence.

ATA - see American Trucking Associations.

automatic slack adjuster - see ABA. A lever connecting the brake chamber pushrod with the foundation brake camshaft. Provides torque to rotate the brake camshaft when the brake treadle is depressed; also provides a means of adjusting clearance between brake shoes and the drum to compensate for lining wear.

automatic traction control (ATC) - an optional system that is available on 4- and 6-channel ABS systems. Automatic traction control minimizes wheel slipping during acceleration by controlling both the engine throttle and brake pressures.

--b--

backing plate - component to which the brake shoes, wheel cylinder and related components are attached.

balance - condition of equal brake pressure distribution within a brake system.

bell-mouthed drum - drum with variation of inner diameter (i.e., greater at open end), preventing full contact with brake lining.

bearing - part that supports and reduces friction between a stationary and moving part or two moving parts.

bearing race - machined surface of a bearing assembly against which the needles, balls or rollers ride. The outer race is also called a cup.

bleeder valve - valve located on disc brake calipers, wheel cylinders and some master cylinders that allows air and fluid to be removed from the brake system.

blue drum - brake drum with friction surface 'blued' from high temperature. High temperature may result, for example, from dragging of brakes caused by weak return springs. Blue drum also may result from lack of brake balance.

boiling point - temperature at which a liquid turns to a vapor.

brake adjuster - see slack adjuster.

brake balance - brake balance is achieved when all brakes on all axles do their fair share of the work.

brake block - the friction material or lining that is attached to a brake shoe. Disc brakes use pads with friction material.

brake chamber - device inside which a diaphragm converts air pressure to mechanical force, via a pushrod, for brake actuation.

brake chamber diaphragm - bellows-type device within brake chamber that converts air pressure to mechanical force via a pushrod.

brake drag - failure of one or more brakes to release immediately and/or completely after a driver removes his foot from the brake treadle (see quick release valve). Constant drag, unrelated to a brake application, also can exist.

Glossary of Terms

brake drum - round cast iron housing attached to an axle shaft or spindle, on which the brake shoes press to stop its rotation.

brake fade - there are many types and causes of brake fade. It may result, for example, from a reduction in friction between linings and drums caused by exposure to water. Most typically, however, fade involves a reduction in braking force experienced when dragging brakes on a long grade. If brakes are misadjusted, an overheated drum may expand to the degree that pushrod travel is insufficient to fully actuate the brakes. This is one example of mechanical fade, which also may result from various mechanical defects (e.g., scored drums) within the foundation brake system. In contrast, heat fade occurs when linings overheat and become less aggressive. Gradual and predictable fade is desirable as a warning.

brake fluid - hydraulic fluid used to transmit hydraulic pressure through the brake lines in a brake system.

brake flushing - procedure to clean the brake hydraulic system with fresh, clean fluid that should be performed whenever new parts are installed.

brake hoses - flexible hoses that connect the brake lines on the chassis with the calipers or wheel cylinders, or the junction block on a solid axle.

brake in - slow wearing in process between two mating part surfaces.

brake pads - see disc brake pads.

brake roller - hardware attached to the bottom of a brake shoe that rides on the brake S-cam.

brake shoes - friction material that is bonded or riveted to curved metal structures and attached to the backing plate by means of brake hardware. The brake shoes press on the brake drum to stop its rotation.

breakaway valve - component that separates the tractor air system from the trailer air system when the tractor air pressure drops below a specified point.

brake proportioning - optional safety-oriented system, often called 'bobtail proportioning,' for limiting drive axle brakes while a tractor is operated without a trailer. Also, a system that varies individual axle braking effort in response to weight or other variable.

brake treadle - the brake pedal; a mechanical lever attached to the foot brake valve.

burnish - to condition or 'season' a brake lining and establish a uniform contact surface between the lining and drum or rotor by means of a test procedure or in-service operation.

---*c*---

caliper - in a disc brake system, the clamping device containing friction material mounted to pads. When actuated, the caliper applies braking force to both sides of the rotor.

castellated nut - nut with slots through which a cotter pin can be passed to secure the nut to its bolt or stud.

castellations - slots cut in a bolt head or on nut flanges, through which a cotter pin is inserted to secure the fastener.

channel/ABS - the number of channels in an individual-wheel-control system refers to the number of individual brakes its electronic control unit (ECU) is capable of independently controlling.

2-channel ABS - a system design that uses two wheel-speed sensors and one control valve. The ABS monitors wheel speed and avoids wheel lock-up on one axle while braking on low-friction surfaces or in emergency situations by rapidly cycling the brakes on the wheel ends of two axles. Commonly used on trailers. This system is the most economical but provides the least control of all ABS systems.

4-channel ABS - a system design that uses four wheel-speed sensors and four ABS control valves on a two-axle truck or tractor. A 4-channel system can also be used on a three-axle vehicle, controlling the left and right side drive axle wheels in pairs. This popular system offers an optimum blend of performance and economy.

6-channel ABS - a system design that features six wheel-speed sensors and six ABS control valves to individually monitor and control all six wheels of a three-axle truck or tractor. This type of system provides the highest available level of ABS control.

check-valve - a one-way check-valve is used, for example, to prevent air from bleeding back into a reservoir. A two-way check-valve activates selectively; for instance, by drawing air for brake application from the most-highly-pressurized reservoir (primary or secondary).

clevis pin - pin connecting the arm of a slack adjuster to a brake chamber pushrod yoke.

Glossary of Terms

combination valve - single unit in the hydraulic brake system that incorporates the metering and proportioning valves in conjunction with the pressure differential switch. Combination valves are categorized as being either two-function or three-function devices, depending on the number of functions they perform. A three-function valve provides all of the aforementioned capabilities of metering, proportioning and warning. However, the two-function unit combines either the proportioning and warning light functions or the metering and warning light operations into a single component.

combination vehicle - truck that is coupled with one or more trailers.

compensating port - opening between the master cylinder bore and reservoir that allows brake fluid to return to the reservoir.

connectors/ABS - sealed, corrosion-resistant plugs that link the ABS wiring system to the electronic control unit (ECU), wheel-speed sensors and modulator or relay valves using a shielded wiring harness.

control algorithm - computer commands programmed into the ECU to control brake actuation under impending wheel lock-up.

cracked drum - brake drum cracked all the way through by excessive heat build-up (perhaps signifying inadequate drum weight, and/or driver abuse and/or resurfacing of a drum beyond the manufacturer's limit).

crack pressure - minimum air pressure, in pounds per square inch (psi), required to open an air valve.

--d--

dash valves - hand controlled air valves mounted on the instrument panel. Some dash valves are used for the parking brakes, differential lock and tractor protection valve.

data link connector - means through which information about the state of the vehicle control system can be extracted with a scan tool or computer. This information includes actual readouts on each sensor's input circuit and some actuator signals. It also can be used to retrieve stored trouble codes.

Department Of Transportation (DOT) - bureau established to assure the coordinated, effective administration of transportation programs and to develop national standardized transportation policies.

diagnostic trouble code (DTC) - code that represents and can be used to identify a malfunction in a computer control system.

diagnostics/ABS - a component-by-component self-check performed each time the truck's ignition is turned on. An independent microprocessor checks the system continuously during vehicle operation.

diagonal system/ABS - a brake system design that divides the ABS into two circuits (the front wheel on one side with rear wheel on the other side, and vice versa) to allow partial system function should one diagonal malfunction.

dial caliper - precision measuring instrument capable of taking inside, outside, depth and step measurements.

dial indicator - measuring device equipped with a readout dial used most often to determine end motion or irregularities.

diaphragm - flexible, impermeable membrane on which pressure acts to produce mechanical movement.

digital - a voltage signal that uses on and off pulses.

digital multimeter (DMM) - instrument that measures volts, ohms and amps and displays the results in numerical form.

digital processing/ABS - the latest processing technology that is many times faster and more reliable than analog processing.

disc brake - braking system that uses cast iron discs mounted on the wheel hubs, over which brake calipers are mounted. Hydraulic or air pressure from the brake system forces the caliper piston(s) against friction pads mounted in the calipers, which in turn clamp the brake discs, stopping their rotation.

disc brake caliper - hydraulic or air actuated device in a disc brake system that is mounted straddling the brake disc. The caliper contains at least one piston and is used to provide clamping force of the brake pads on the disc.

disc brake pads - friction material that is bonded or riveted to metal plates and mounted in the disc brake caliper. The brake pads are clamped against the disc brake rotor to stop its rotation.

disc brake rotor - cast iron disc mounted on the wheel hub, which is clamped by the caliper and disc brake pads to slow and stop its rotation.

directional stability - the ability of a truck to travel in a straight line on a flat surface with a minimum of driver control.

DOT - see Department of Transportation.

drain valve - used to drain oil and water from wet tank; valve may be manual or automatic in operation. Automatic versions, which may be heated electrically to prevent the valve freezing open, often are referred to as spitter valves.

Driver Vehicle Inspection Report (DVIR) – used by the driver to identify defects or deficiencies that would result in a mechanical breakdown or effect the safe operation of a vehicle. DVIR is submitted to the motor carrier dialer for follow up repairs to the vehicle.

DTC - see diagnostic trouble code.

dual brake system - a dual air system-primary and secondary-designed to retain braking ability in the event one system fails.

dual master cylinder - master cylinder that has one cylinder bore, but two pistons and two fluid reservoirs. Each piston applies hydraulic pressure to two wheels only. In the event one of the hydraulic circuits fails, the other provides enough braking power to stop the vehicle.

duplex gauge - essentially, a diagnostic device incorporating two separate air gauges with a common housing and utilizing indicator needles of different colors. A duplex gauge may be used to diagnose brake system imbalance within a combination vehicle by means of simultaneous connection to two points (such as the tractor gladhand and a trailer brake chamber).

dust shield - plate made of metal or polyethylene that's mounted behind a brake drum to minimizes entry of dirt and road splash.

--*e*--

ECU/ABS - electronic control unit; a microprocessor that evaluates how fast a wheel is rotating. The electrical signals generated by the inductive sensors pick up impulses from toothed rings that spin with the wheel.

edge codes - developed by Friction Materials Standards Institute, a double letter code (e.g., EE, FF, GG, FG) printed on the edge of a brake block to designate its range of aggressiveness.

electronic control module (ECM) - microprocessor that is used to monitor and control electronic engine controls.

emergency brake system - not a separate system; emergency braking (in the event of air loss) involves various portions of the parking and service brake systems (see parking brake).

Environmental Protection Agency (EPA) - U.S. agency that ensures that Federal environmental laws are implemented and effectively enforced.

--*f*--

fail-safe/ABS - dash light warns driver that ABS is disengaged if anti-lock brake system fails during vehicle operation. Meanwhile, the tractor's pneumatic system returns to normal relay valve functions and maintains standard air brake performance.

fault codes/ABS - a series of codes displayed by the self-diagnostic portion of the ABS unit, isolating the section of the system that is malfunctioning or has malfunctioned.

Federal Highway Administration (FHWA) - Department of Transportation (DOT) agency that administers federal highway funding and implements regulations, policies and guidelines for safety, access and development of U.S. highways.

Federal Motor Carrier Safety Administration (FMCSA) - Department of Transportation (DOT) agency that establishes and enforces safety regulations regarding commercial motor vehicles.

Federal Motor Vehicle Safety Standards (FMVSS) - Department of Transportation (DOT) standards a vehicle must meet before it is produced for the consumer.

fixed caliper - brake caliper design that contains one or two pistons positioned on either side of the rotor. The caliper is rigidly attached to the spindle and the pads are applied with equal hydraulic or air pressure from both sides.

flare - expanded, shaped end on a metal tube or pipe.

floating caliper - brake caliper design that uses an adapter, or anchor plate, which is bolted to the spindle. The caliper floats laterally across a pair of special bolts that are screwed into the adapter. As hydraulic or air pressure is applied to the piston, the inboard pad is forced against the rotor. This pressure causes the caliper to move inboard until an equal pressure is applied by the outside pad to the outer disc surface.

fluid - something that flows; both liquids and gases are fluids.

flush - to remove foreign material from the brake system by forcing brake fluid through the lines.

foot pound - unit of measurement for torque. One foot pound is the torque obtained by a force of one pound applied to a wrench handle that is 12-in. long; a unit of energy required to raise a weight of one pound, a distance of one foot.

foot valve - a foot-operated valve that controls air pressure delivered to the brake chambers.

force - pushing effort measured in pounds; the form of energy that puts an object at rest into motion or changes the motion of a moving object.

foundation brake system - includes mechanical components involved in providing braking force: brake chambers, slack adjusters, brake drums and brake linings.

--g--

galling - weld-like damage to a metal due to lack of lubrication.

gasket - material such as artificial rubber, cork, or steel used to seal between parts.

GCW - gross combination weight; the total weight-carrying capacity of a combination vehicle as determined by axle ratings.

gladhand - mechanical connector used to attach a tractor or converter dolly's service (control) and emergency (supply) air lines to those on a trailer.

grease-stained drum - a brake drum with discoloration of the friction surface caused by, for example, improper greasing of the brake camshaft.

GVW - gross vehicle weight; the total weight-carrying capacity of one vehicle (e.g., straight truck, bus, tractor or trailer) as determined by axle ratings.

--h--

Hall effect - when current flows through a thin wafer of semiconductor material, and a magnetic field crosses it at a right angle, a voltage known as a Hall effect voltage will be generated at the edge of the material. Interrupting the magnetic field turns off the voltage. This is the principle used by Hall effect sensors.

hand valve - see trailer control valve.

heat-checked drum - brake drum with hairline cracks on the friction surface caused by thermal cycling. Mild checking normally does not require replacement of the drum.

heat-spotted drum - a brake drum that exhibits a pattern of hard, slightly raised dark spots of martensite on its friction surface. Caused by localized overheating and sudden cooling, those spots should be ground off to prevent drum cracking, uneven line wear and loss of braking efficiency. If the spots cannot be removed, the drum should be discarded. Heat spotting is promoted by light and steady braking on downgrades.

heavy-duty truck - truck with a 26,001 lb. or more Gross Vehicle Weight (GVW).

hold-off spring - a spring within a relay valve or quick release valve that is designed to retard valve operation until a pre-determined amount of air pressure is exerted (see crack pressure).

hub - mounting point for the wheel on an axle or spindle; the part of the synchronizer assembly that is splined to the transmission shaft; the center part of a wheel, gear, etc., that rides on a shaft.

hydraulic brakes - brakes that are engaged by hydraulic pressure.

hydro-boost - power brake system that uses power steering pump fluid pressure rather than intake manifold vacuum.

hygroscopic - the ability of a material or substance to attract water.

hysteresis - difference between the amount of pressure needed to open a valve and the pressure drop needed to close it.

--i--

ID - acronym for inside diameter.

Glossary of Terms

inner bearing race - inner part of a ball or roller bearing that provides a surface for the balls or rollers to rotate.

integral ABS - anti-lock braking system that substitutes the traditional master cylinder and power booster with a self-contained modulator and high-pressure accumulator.

inversion valve - an air control valve, normally open, often used in interlocking applications where components must operate in a specific sequence.

--j--

jackknife - uncontrollable articulation of a tractor-trailer, typically resulting from lock-up of tractor drive axle(s). The risk of jackknifing is greatest on a slippery road with an empty or lightly-laden trailer in tow.

Jake Brake® - the trademark of engine brakes manufactured by the Vehicle Equipment Division of The Jacobs Manufacturing Co.

jam nut - locknut.

--l--

leakdown test - method of checking for air leaks. With engine off, vehicle stationary, air system at maximum governed pressure and all service brakes fully applied, there should be no more than a 3 psi/minimum air loss noted on a dash-mounted pressure gauge for straight trucks; 4 psi/minimum for combination vehicles.

Less-Than-Truckload (LTL) - freight that is less than what is required to fill a trailer (usually less than 10,000 lb.).

lining growth - permanent swelling of brake lining resulting from heat exposure.

long-stroke chamber - a brake chamber designed to permit longer-than-normal pushrod travel without exceeding its readjustment limit. For example, a regular, clamp-type, Type-30 chamber has a readjustment limit of 2-in.; the long-stroke version of that chamber has a readjustment limit of 21/2-in.

low pressure warning device - pressure-sensitive electrical switch that actuates an in-cab buzzer and warning light when air pressure falls below a predetermined level (typically 60 psi).

--m--

metering valve - valve used on front disc/rear drum brake systems for the purpose of providing a simultaneous application of the front and rear friction materials. Located in the front brake hydraulic circuit, the metering valve delays front disc brake operation until the rear brakes shoes overcome the return spring tension.

micrometer - precision measuring instrument. When a micrometer measures in thousandths of an inch, one turn of its thimble results in 0.025-in. movement of its spindle.

microprocessor - portion of a microcomputer that receives sensor input and handles calculations.

millimeter - the base of metric size measurement. One millimeter equals 0.039370-in. One inch is equal to 25.4 mm.

modulator - component in the ABS system that contains the solenoid valves that regulate pressure to the service brakes.

--n--

National Institute for Automotive Service Excellence (ASE, formerly NIASE) - nonprofit certification agency for automotive, truck, school bus, auto body, engine machine shop and parts personnel.

National Highway Traffic Safety Administration (NHTSA) - Department of Transportation (DOT) agency established to carry out safety programs. NHTSA investigates safety defects in motor vehicles, sets and enforces fuel economy standards, helps states and local communities reduce the threat of drunk drivers, promotes the use of safety belts, child safety seats and air bags, investigates odometer fraud, establishes and enforces vehicle anti-theft regulations and provides consumer information on motor vehicle safety topics.

normal wear - average expected wear when operating under normal conditions.

--o--

Occupational Safety and Health Administration (OSHA) - adopts and enforces health and safety standards in the workplace.

OD - acronym for outside diameter.

OEM - acronym for Original Equipment Manufacturer.

Glossary of Terms

out-of-round drum - brake drum with variation in its inner diameter, causing reduced braking efficiency. Some out-of-round drums can be machined, within manufacturer's limits, to restore concentricity.

oversized drum - refers to a brake drum having an inner diameter greater than the discard diameter marked on the drum by its manufacturer.

--*p*--

parking brake - system that applies the brakes mechanically through a series of linkages and cables. Depending on the vehicle, the parking brake system will either be actuated using a foot pedal or a hand-operated lever.

parking brake priority - a trailer brake control valve, which prioritizes delivery of air for quick release of a trailer's parking brakes after being hooked to a tractor. Charging a trailer's service reservoirs to provide braking ability is a secondary concern.

pawl - a mechanical device allowing rotation in only one direction. One type consists of a hinged tongue, the tip of which engages the notches of a cogwheel, preventing backward motion.

piston - cylindrical component that is attached to the connecting rod and moves up-and-down in the air compressor.

piston head - part of the piston that is above the rings.

piston ring - open-ended ring that fits into a groove on the outer diameter of the piston. Its chief function is to form a seal between the piston and cylinder wall.

pneumatic balance - achieved when individual air chambers receive the air pressure required for each brake in the system to do its fair share of the work. Lack of pneumatic balance is most likely at low brake application pressures, but rare during panic stops.

pneumatic timing balance - achieved when individual air chambers sequentially receive air within a time frame that ensures each brake in the system will do its fair share of the work. In a combination vehicle, lack of proper timing is likely to occur because tractor brakes receive air faster than trailer brakes (see trailer push).

polished drums - a brake drum with a friction surface polished to a mirror-like finish by unsuitable brake linings. Remove drum gloss with 80 grit emery cloth.

pop-off valve - jargon for a pressure-relief valve, installed in the service reservoir or wet tanks as insurance against over-pressurization.

power booster - device that uses a diaphragm, engine vacuum and atmospheric pressure to assist the driver with brake application. Also known as a vacuum booster.

pressure differential - difference between the inlet and outlet air pressure of an open brake valve. Also, difference in air pressure between any two points within a brake system.

primary shoe - brake shoe in a duo-servo drum brake system that transfers part of its force to the secondary shoe. The brake shoe facing the front of the vehicle when the vehicle is moving forward.

proportioning valve - proportioning valve is used to control hydraulic pressure to the rear brakes. When the pressure to the rear brakes reaches a predetermined level, the proportioning valve overcomes the force of its spring-loaded piston and stops the flow of fluid to the rear brakes. This action maintains rear brake system pressure at a lower level than the front brakes, keeping the rear brakes from locking during hard stops.

psi - measurement of pressure in pounds per square inch.

pumping the brakes - a rapid series of brake applications (also known as 'fanning') used to avoid locking brakes on axles during sudden stops. The phrase also may apply to a slower series of heavy brake applications (also known as 'snubbing') used in an attempt to prevent brake overheating on long downgrades.

pushrod - a rod, protruding from a brake chamber, which is connected to the arm of a slack adjuster via a clevis pin.

--*q*--

quick-release valve - device that allows brake actuation air to be quickly exhausted near the brakes it serves, rather than having to travel back through the supply line.

quick take-up master cylinder - master cylinder design that is used to prevent excessive brake pedal travel. The quick take-up master cylinder uses a larger rear cylinder bore and quick take-up valve. This arrangement provides a large volume of fluid at low pressure (light pedal application) during the initial part of the pedal stroke. Also called a step-bore master cylinder.

Glossary of Terms

quick take-up valve - valve used in a quick take-up master cylinder that controls fluid flow into the reservoir.

--r--

race - channel in the inner or outer ring of an anti-friction bearing in which the balls or rollers operate.

radio frequency interference (RFI) - the external interference of false signals from such sources as radar, citizens' band (CB) radios, and other types of radio transmissions and television signals. While the effect of this interference on ABS was a concern during the 1970s, today's technology has virtually eliminated the problem.

ratio-limiting value - prevents locking of front brakes by automatically limiting application pressure to steer axle during normal braking. Progressively harder braking, however, will progressively increase steer-axle braking until maximum torque is applied.

relay valve - used to speed application of brakes, especially in multiple-trailer applications.

release time - the time between release of brake treadle and total disengagement of brake linings and brake drums. Or, per Federal Motor Vehicle Safety Standard (FMVSS) 121, the time required to reduce pressure to 5 psi from 95 psi within all service chambers.

retarder - an auxiliary braking device, such as an engine brake, exhaust brake, hydraulic retarder or electric retarder.

return springs - springs that retract brake shoes upon release of the brake treadle.

roll-over - jargon denoting that an S-cam has traveled beyond its designed stopping position during brake application.

runout - wobble or deflection beyond a rotating part's normal plane of movement.

--s--

scan tool - microprocessor designed to communicate with a vehicle's on-board computer system to perform diagnostic and troubleshooting functions.

scan tool data - information from the vehicle computer that is displayed on the scan tool. This data includes component and system values on the data stream, DTCs, and on some systems, freeze frame data, system monitors and readiness monitors.

secondary shoe - brake shoe in a duo-servo drum brake system that receives force from the primary shoe when the brakes are applied. The secondary shoe does most of the braking when the vehicle is traveling forward, so its lining is larger than that of the primary shoe.

S-cam brake - type of brake where mechanically-induced rotation of an S-shaped cam forces brake linings against the brake drum.

scored drum - brake drum with a grooved friction surface, resulting in excessive lining wear. Severe scoring requires that a drum be machined, within manufacturer's limits, before replacing the linings.

self-diagnostics - refers to the way in which the computer control system constantly monitors the state of each of its sensors and actuators. If one of them produces an implausible signal, or no signal at all, the system registers a fault code.

sending unit - mechanical, electrical, hydraulic or electro-mechanical device, which transmits information to a gauge or other receiving unit.

sensor - any mechanism by which the computer can measure some variable, such as engine speed. Each sensor works by sending the computer a signal of some sort, a coded electronic message that corresponds to some point on the range of the variable measured by that sensor.

service brakes - as opposed to parking brakes; the portion of the brake system used for normal brake applications.

service brake priority - a type of trailer brake control valve, which prioritizes delivery of air to a trailer's service reservoirs, to provide braking ability, after being hooked to a tractor. Releasing a trailer's parking brakes is a secondary concern.

slack adjuster - also called a brake adjuster; a lever connecting the brake chamber pushrod with the foundation brake camshaft. It provides torque to rotate the brake camshaft when the brake treadle is depressed, and provides a means of adjusting clearance between brake shoes and the drum to compensate for lining wear. Some models are automatic while others require manual adjustment.

sliding caliper - brake caliper design that operates similarly to the floating design, however, it attaches to the anchor plate using only one attachment point.

speed sensor/ABS - an electromagnetic device that, in conjunction with a rotating toothed wheel, generates an electrical signal proportional to the wheel speed and transmit the information to the ABS electronic control unit (ECU).

spitter valve - see drain valve.

split-coefficient surface - a road condition where one side of a lane has low friction and the other has high friction (e.g., the left side of the lane is covered with ice, but the right side is dry). Also called a split-m ('mu') surface. A 4- or 6-channel ABS (anti-lock brake system) with individual wheel control will provide optimum stability and stopping distance performance under these conditions.

spring brake - generally refers to a tandem-chamber brake actuator that incorporates an air-applied service brake chamber and an air-release/spring-applied parking or emergency brake chamber. Spring brakes apply upon sudden air loss (emergency mode) or activation of a dash-mounted parking brake control. Spring brakes remain applied until that chamber is recharged with air or the spring is manually compressed or caged.

WARNING: DISASSEMBLY OF A SPRING BRAKE IS DANGEROUS! ONLY TRAINED TECHNICIANS SHOULD ATTEMPT THE PROCEDURE!

The spring portion often is referred to as the piggy-back. Some spring brake actuators do not incorporate a service air chamber and are only parking and emergency brakes. For example, some parking brakes are applied by air pressure and subsequently held mechanically by a pin, which drops into a notch on the brake chamber pushrod.

stopping distance - distance traveled by a vehicle on a road between the initial brake application and a full stop.

stopping time - time elapsed between the initial brake application and a full stop.

stroke - refers to the total distance traveled by a brake chamber pushrod or slack adjuster arm during brake application.

supply air tank - air reservoir immediately downstream of the air compressor (see wet tank).

--t--

tandem axles - two single-axle assemblies, one behind the other.

taper - gradual decrease in width or thickness; the difference in diameter between the cylinder bore at the bottom of the hole and the bore at the top of the hole, just below the ridge.

technical service bulletin (TSB) - information published by vehicle manufacturers that describes updated service procedures and service procedures that should be used to handle vehicle defects.

Technology and Maintenance Council (TMC) - formerly named The Maintenance Council. Branch of the American Trucking Associations dedicated to providing technology solutions to the trucking industry through education, networking and standards development.

threaded drum - brake drum improperly resurfaced on a lathe, resulting in a friction surface akin to that of a scored drum.

tire rolling radius - the distance, expressed in inches, from the center of a tire/wheel assembly to the pavement, measured when mounted on a vehicle and loaded to its maximum rated capacity.

torque balance - achieved when individual brakes exert the degree of braking force required for each brake in the system to do its fair share of the work.

tractor - truck that pulls a trailer using a fifth wheel mounted over the rear axles.

tractor protection valve - isolates tractor air system in the event of a trailer breakaway or dangerous decrease in the tractor's reserve air, but is typically applied (via dash-mounted control) before disconnecting a trailer.

tractor trailer - tractor and trailer combination.

trailer control valve - hand-operated valve, located on (or adjacent to) the steering column, which permits independent control of the trailer brakes. Also known as the trolley valve or hand valve.

trailer push - caused by the tractor braking prior to the trailer and/or with greater torque.

trailer swing - articulation of the trailer caused by locking only the trailer brakes.

Glossary of Terms

treadle valve - foot-operated brake actuation valve.

trolley valve - see trailer control valve.

Truck Trailer Manufacturers Association (TTMA) - agency that establishes and maintains relationships between manufacturers of truck trailers, cargo tanks, internodal containers and their suppliers.

turned drum - a brake drum that has been resurfaced on a lathe to remove scoring or other defects. Always be sure to stay within manufacturer's limits when turning a drum.

--v--

vacuum booster - device that uses a diaphragm, engine vacuum and atmospheric pressure to assist the driver with brake application. Also known as a power booster.

valve - device that controls the pressure, direction or rate of flow of a liquid or air.

Vehicle Identification Number (VIN) - combination of numbers and letters unique to each vehicle that identifies certain characteristics of the vehicle.

vehicle speed sensor (VSS) - permanent magnet sensor, usually located on the transmission, which provides an input to the vehicle computer control system regarding vehicle speed.

voltage - electrical pressure which causes current flow in a circuit.

--w--

warning light - an indicator light on the truck or tractor instrument panel that illuminates to indicate the status of the ABS system. On trailer ABS, the indicator light may be located on the trailer body where it can easily be seen by the driver or maintenance personnel.

wet tank - the reservoir nearest to the air compressor, where water and oil are most likely to accumulate (assuming the lack of a functional air dryer). Also known as the supply air tank.

wheel cylinder - cylinder connected to a drum brake hydraulic system. Hydraulic pressure in the system applies piston(s) in the wheel cylinder against the brake shoes, forcing the shoes against the inside of the brake drum and stopping its rotation.

worm gear - a component of the slack adjuster. The worm and worm gear provide for adjusting lining-to-drum clearance.

--y--

yaw rate sensor – gyroscopic velocity sensor that measures understeer or oversteer of a vehicle.

Notes